WORD

FOR EVERY

DAY

OF THE

YEAR

STEVEN POOLE

Quercus

First published hardback in Great Britain in 2019 by Quercus Editions Ltd

This paperback edition published in Great Britain in 2020 by

Quercus Editions Ltd
Carmelite House
50 Victoria Embankment
London EC4Y 0DZ

An Hachette UK company

A CIP catalogue record for this book is available
from the British Library

PB ISBN 978 1 78747 858 9
Ebook ISBN 978 1 78747 859 6

Every effort has been made to contact copyright holders.
However, the publishers will be glad to rectify in future editions
any inadvertent omissions brought to their attention.

Quercus Editions Ltd hereby exclude all liability to the extent permitted
by law for any errors or omissions in this book and for any loss, damage
or expense (whether direct or indirect) suffered by a third party
relying on any information contained in this book.

10 9 8 7 6 5 4 3

Typeset by CC Book Production
Printed and bound in Great Britain by Clays Ltd, Elcograf S.p.A.

MIX
Paper from
responsible sources
FSC® C104740

Papers used by Quercus Editions Ltd are from well-managed forests and other responsible sources.

for V. J.

Author's Note

William Morris said that you should keep 'nothing in your house that you do not know to be useful or believe to be beautiful', and that principle has also guided the construction of this little house of words.

Most of the terms gathered here are old and half-forgotten, or thoroughly forgotten; but human nature has not changed very much over the first millennium of the English language, and civilization has hardly outgrown the ancient, and wonderfully exact, words for particular ways in which people can excel or err, deceive themselves and others, or just be very annoying. Many of these words, too, capture a specific sense not otherwise available in modern vocabulary. We could do worse than enrich our speech with such long-buried gems.

With a few irresistible exceptions, I have generally avoided including words that belong in two categories. The first is what dictionaries call *nonce-words*: these are words coined once, whether seriously or in jest, that never caught on – for which, indeed, there is no evidence of their ever having been used a second time.* The second category is

---

* The very old word *nonce* here carries the sense of *for the nonce*, 'for a particular occasion': *nonce-word* itself, coined by the *OED*'s first editor, James Murray, did not itself prove to be a nonce-word.

what one might call *dictionary orphans*: words that, having appeared in one old dictionary, are copied and repeated in successive lexicons down the ages, without ever being used in anger by a writer trying to communicate a thought. Both these categories are very commonly found in miscellanies of interesting words, but such words cannot honestly said to have really entered the language. The great majority of the following, on the other hand, did – and might, with your help, do so again.

S. P., London, August 2019

January

1 JANUARY

Dringle

One may be forgiven on New Year's Day for *dringling*, after the excesses of the night before. To *dringle* is to 'waste time in a lazy lingering manner', according to the English philologist Robert Forby, a scholar and rector of Fincham in Norfolk. Five years after his death, in 1830, his mammoth work *The Vocabulary of East Anglia: An Attempt to Record the Vulgar Tongue of the Twin Sister Counties, Norfolk and Suffolk, As It Existed In the Last Twenty Years of the Eighteenth Century, and Still Exists; With Proof of Its Antiquity from Etymology and Authority* was finally published. (Do not suppose that the reverend Forby had been *dringling* when he composed this title.)

The verb *dringle* is attested from 1680, when it was said of some wretch that he was 'Condemn'd to endure the Fatigues of Life to the last dringling Sand'. Its etymology is uncertain, but Forby assures his readers that its meaning is close to that of *drumble*, 'to dawdle'. In Shakespeare's *The Merry Wives of Windsor*, Mrs Ford berates the servants for their sluggishness in carrying off the laundry basket by exclaiming: 'Look how you drumble!' Forby assures us: 'Had that merry gossip been an East Angle, she must have said *dringle*.'

2 January

Obnubilate

In Thomas Blount's *Glossographia* of 1656 we find this lovely definition: '*Obnubilate* ... to make clouds, or dark with clouds, to make heavy and sad in countenance.' *Nubilum* is the Latin for cloud, and so *obnubilate* was adopted for 'to darken' from 1583, when the pamphleteer Philip Stubbes railed against the decadence of his age in *The Anatomie of Abuses*. Among the vicious habits Stubbes decried, including licentiousness and drinking, was women's use of perfume. Just as 'mists and exhalations which evaporate from these earthly bodies ... do rather *obnubilate* and darken the beams of the sun,' Stubbes explained, 'so these (in a manner) palpable odors, fumes, vapours, smells of these musks, civets, pomanders, perfumes, balms and such like, ascending to the brain, do rather denigrate, darken, and obscure the spirit and senses, than either lighten them, or comfort them any manner of way'. Well, that told them.

In the novel *The Mauritius Command* (1977), surgeon Stephen Maturin is upbraided for his opium habit: 'It is the pity of the world, Dr. Maturin, to see a man of your parts *obnubilate* his mind with the juice of the poppy.' The book is part of the Master and Commander series by Patrick O'Brian, who died on this day in 2000.

4

Eucatastrophe

J. R. R. Tolkien, born on this day in 1892, was sad that the English language lacked a term for an unexpected, sudden happy ending, so he proposed *eucatastrophe*. As he explained in a 1944 letter, he means 'the sudden happy turn in a story which pierces you with a joy that brings tears'. Tolkien thought it particularly useful in a religious context: 'The Birth of Christ is the eucatastrophe of Man's history,' he wrote later. 'The Resurrection is the eucatastrophe of the story of the Incarnation.'

But hang on: isn't a catastrophe something bad? That is indeed the way it is used in modern English, but – as Tolkien very well knew – it comes from the Greek for 'sudden turn' or 'conclusion', and once meant merely the dénouement of a dramatic piece, before it acquired the sense of, as Dr Johnson puts it, 'a conclusion generally unhappy', and then any kind of very bad event. For us moderns, then, the idea of a *eucatastrophe* or 'good catastrophe' has an extra pleasant tang of paradox that might recommend its resurrection.

Malversation

This word sounds like it ought to mean 'bad chat' or 'incompetent conversation', and indeed both *malversation* and *conversation* share the Latin root *versari* ('to be, act, or dwell'). But whereas *conversation* etymologically means 'to turn oneself about' and thereby 'to interact with others', *malversation* means 'to act wrongly'. Specifically, in English since the sixteenth century, *malversation* is corrupt administration by one in high office.

It was a word not lost on T. S. Eliot, who died on this day in 1965. In his verse drama *Murder in the Cathedral* (1935), about the assassination of Thomas à Becket during the reign of Henry II, a priest remarks: 'I see nothing quite conclusive in the art of temporal government, / But violence, duplicity and frequent *malversation.*' Plus ça change.

Kickshaw

Tonight being the twelfth and final night of Christmas, let us indulge in some *kickshaws*. The original meaning of *kickshaw* was a fancy French dish, as opposed to honest and substantial English fare. As so, it was also applied to any trivial or ridiculous thing, as in *Twelfth Night* itself, when Sir Andrew asserts his 'delight in Masques and Revels sometimes altogether', to which Sir Toby asks in response: 'Art thou good at these *kickshawses*, Knight?'

Authorities agree that the English word is a simple corruption of the French *quelque chose*, 'something', but, as Dr Johnson observes: 'Milton seems to have understood it otherwise; for he writes it *kickshoe*, and seems to think it used in contempt of dancing.' (Milton was worried that having young English men educated in Paris would transform them into 'mimicks, apes, and kickshoes'; the spelling *kickshoe* continued to be not uncommon, even when applied to food.) Among the last uses recorded in the *OED* is by Dickens in *The Mystery of Edwin Drood*, when Mr Jasper at the piano sings 'no kickshaw ditties' but 'the genuine George the Third home-brewed', i.e. proper English music. Since there is no shortage of the frivolous or ridiculous today, it could still come in useful.

6 January

Palmary

Speakers of English are constantly inventing new ways to call something excellent, bodacious, bad, dope, or sick, which phenomenon in itself is rather cause for optimism, since there would be no need for such continuous linguistic invention if everything really were as bad as it seemed. One could do worse, in this line of endeavour, than to resurrect some lovely old terms that have fallen out of use, and one such is *palmary*, attested since 1646.

In ancient Rome, the winner in a sporting competition was awarded the palm leaf, and so Latin *palmarius* means 'that which bears off the palm of victory'; or, generally, 'superlative'. So too *palmary* in English: it can mean 'chief' or 'pre-eminent' (as in 'the palmary reason to do something'), 'excellent', or simply the best. The lawyer John Cook, who led the prosecution of Charles I after Parliament set up the court on this day in 1649, used it in defence of the English legal system. 'Beyond Sea,' he observed in *The Vindication of the Professors and Profession of the Law* (1641), 'you cannot peep into an Advocate's study but he cries give, give, and if the Cause go for his Client then he hath his *Palmary* Fee, in token of Victory.' Cook's own fee for his work, unfortunately, was execution upon the restoration of the crown.

Ultracrepidarian

Apelles was a famous painter in fourth-century Athens BCE, who used to exhibit his paintings in the marketplace and then hide himself while eavesdropping on what people said about them. On one occasion, he heard a cobbler remark that the sandal in the picture lacked a loop, so Apelles painted on a new one overnight. The next day, however, the same cobbler now said there was something wrong with the subject's leg. Apelles emerged from the shadows and rebuked him majestically thus: 'Cobbler, do not go higher than your shoe.'

In Latin, this gave rise to the phrase *ultra crepidam* – 'beyond the sole' – and so in English to *ultracrepidarian*: one who opines beyond his expertise. In this form it was coined by Coleridge, but the bishop Joseph Henshaw had, in 1640, denounced 'those *ultra-crepitasts* [sic] that ... would teach Saint Paul divinity'. The writer Samuel Roffey Maitland, born on this day in 1792, wrote of the literary world in 1837: 'there is among the infinity of anonymous writing, compiling, concocting, editing, and criticising, so much pretence ... so much *ultracrepidizing*, that ... truth may be outfaced by ignorance and falsehood'. One can only imagine what he might have said of our own *ultracrepidarian* age.

8 JANUARY

Zeitgeber

Any regular environmental cue that alerts a living thing to what time of day it is – for instance, the rising of the sun – can be called a *zeitgeber* (pronounced ZITEgaybėr), from the German words for 'time' and 'giver'. The German compound itself was coined in 1954 by the biologist Jürgen Aschoff, who is considered the founder of the field of chronobiology: this is concerned with physiological phenomena that exhibit cycles in time.

In humans, sleep is particularly sensitive to *zeitgeber* (the word is the same in the plural) such as variations in light and temperature, but also 'exercise, food, and social activities', noted a sleep researcher in 2012. Not to mention, of course, devices that show the time. Galileo Galilei – who died on this day in 1642 – created the first design for a pendulum clock; later, Christiaan Huygens built the first one. In a world where everyone feels time-poor, it might make us feel better to adopt the beautiful word *zeitgeber*, which argues that having fun *gives* us time rather than taking it away.

Colophon

An inscription at the end of a book is known as the *colophon*, from the Greek for 'summit'. Its first recorded appearance in English is provided by the literary historian and poet laureate Thomas Warton, born on this day in 1728. In his *History of English Poetry* (1774), he mentions a book recounting the medieval legend of Robert Le Diable, a Norman knight who discovers he is the son of Satan. 'The volume has this *colophon*,' Warton remarks: 'Here endeth the life of the most fearfullest and unmercyfullest and mischievous Robert the devil which was afterwards called the servant of our Lord Jesus Christ. Emprinted in Fleet-street at the sign of the sun by Wynkyn de Worde.'

Modern colophons, alas, are not so dramatic, and liable to tell you, if they exist at all, about the typeface used in the book, which many of us are at least pleased to know, or simply the publisher's name and place of printing. In the book trade, a *colophon* can also be the publisher's sigil or logo: a lighthouse, as it might be, or a puffin. More generally, you may use *colophon* to mean the finishing touch of anything at all.

Indesinent

Arthur Dent, the hero of Douglas Adams's deathless *The Hitch-Hiker's Guide to the Galaxy* (1979), shares his name with Arthur Dent, the sixteenth-century religious writer whose bestselling work was entitled, not unsimilarly, *The Plaine-Mans Path-way to Heaven* (1601). In that work, Dent draws a helpful moral, as was common, from the fact that ants worked so hard: 'What *indesinent* paines, and unwearied labour, this seely [blessed] creature taketh.'

What is *indesinent* (from the Latin for 'not leaving') is unceasing; perhaps because it also calls to mind *indecent*, it seems usually to have been employed for things one would prefer not to mention, or that one might wish did end but don't. The writer Edward Dubois, who died on this day in 1850, used it to amusing effect in his *A Piece of Family Biography* (1799), in which we are told that that one Sir David would not smoke his pipe when visiting the local manor, 'perhaps through fear of offending her ladyship's olfactory nerves', but 'he made up for this loss by an *indesinent* application to his snuff-box'. There being in our time no shortage of things that would be better if finally over and done with, we still need the word.

Fnord

The possibly satirical religion of Discordianism was founded by Greg Hill and Kerry Wendell Thornley in 1963, when the *Principia Discordia* was first printed. It contained the mystical nonsense word *fnord*, which was later taken up by Robert Anton Wilson – who died on this day in 2007 – and Robert Shea in their *Illuminatus!* trilogy. In the world of these novels, children are taught not to be able to see the word *fnord*, but every time it is encountered they will feel unease and fear, and be unable to rationally consider the text it appears in: so the government maintains control over a nervous population.

More generally, a *fnord* has since come to mean any obscure message, surreal event, or unexpected phenomenon, and it is even sometimes used as a placeholder term in computer programming. The phrase 'I have seen the fnords' means that the speaker has come to understand some previously obscured truth about the hidden connections between things. Have you seen the fnords?

12 JANUARY

Roynish

What is *roynish* is vulgar or despicable. (From the English *roin*, a 'scab', in turn perhaps from the Latin for 'red' or 'rusty'.) In Shakespeare's *As You Like It*, a lord calls Touchstone a 'roynish clown', which is perhaps more indicative of the coarseness of lords than of the qualities of this entertainer. Rascals, fashions, and insinuations would all later be called *roynish* through pursed lips.

It was a word employed with particularly gleeful force by Thomas Nashe, the Elizabethan poet, playwright, and controversialist. In his pamphlet *Strange News*, which was registered for publication on this day in 1593, he upbraids his rival, Gabriel Harvey, for what he calls splendidly his 'roisterdoisterdom', and adds: 'with none but clownish and *roynish* jests dost thou rush upon us'. Then as now, spats between writers in public were royal entertainment.

13 January

Acrasia

If you sometimes wake up with the suspicion that you over-indulged the night before, you might have been a temporary victim – as who is not, from time to time? – of *acrasia*: a lack of temperance or self-control. It comes from the Latin *acrasia* meaning 'intemperance', which itself derives from the Greek *acrasia* meaning a 'bad mixture' (e.g. of meats). In the wonderful long poem *The Faerie Queene* by Edmund Spenser – who died on this day in 1599 – Acrasia is personified as an extremely tempting queen from whom radiate sexy eye-beams and who hangs out in a place called the Bower of Bliss, though the rest of her realm is stultified and lazy. At least the hungover reader might feel better about such a temporary abandonment of moderation if it is called by this fine old poetic name.

Fugacious

What is *fugacious* is, by the Latin derivation, apt to flee or fly away, and so fleeting, but it differs from *evanid* (see 22 March) in that things called *fugacious* are usually abstract. So writers have spoken of 'fugacious pleasures', 'fugacious anecdotes', and, in sum, 'the fugacious nature of life and time'. In his 1820 dictionary, *Philology of the English Language*, the playwright and classicist Richard Paul Jodrell, who died on this day in 1861, illustrates it thus: 'He descanted very philosophically, and effused many sage reflections on the *fugaciousness* of connubial felicity, and instability of human enjoyments.' (That is from the Scottish satirist Archibald Campbell's aping of 'affected style' in his 1767 *Lexiphanes*.)

Conversation and pleasure, then, are widely agreed to be *fugacious*, this being all the more reason to treasure them: what is fugacious is usually most valuable. This is true, too, of another sense describing a volatile substance apt to change. So in 1823 one ingenious chap wrote to the *Annals of Philosophy* noting 'the highly *fugacious* nature of that part of coffee on which its fine flavour depends', and suggesting a new method of preparing it, involving a glass vial with a cork stopper, placed in a boiling water bath. Which idea itself was, unfortunately for its inventor, *fugacious*.

Sitzfleisch

If you are able to concentrate on or persist in something for a long time, then you are blessed with *sitzfleisch*. This is German for 'sitting-flesh' and so literally means the buttocks, but was also used to mean perserverance or endurance. So, via Yiddish, it entered the English language in the mid-nineteenth century, when a biographer credited the German orientalist Martin Haug with 'a goodly store of *sitzfleisch*, or power of sedentary endurance'.

Later, a critic for the *Atlantic* in 1971 wrote, rather pissily, of the French composer Olivier Messiaen: 'It takes not only special training but a liberal endowment of Sitzfleisch to hear one of his pieces out from one end to the other.' This is to ignore the indomitable *sitzfleisch* possessed by Messiaen himself, who was taken prisoner by the Germans in 1940, and whose stunning *Quartet for the End of Time* was premiered on this day in 1941, in the Stalag VIII-A camp.

Quisquilian

The Latin plural *quisquilae*, 'a reduplicative form of uncertain origin' (*OED*), seems literally to mean something like 'this or that', and was used to denote rubbish or garbage. So *quisquilian*, or *quisquilious*, means worthless. It comes – as so many insults, pleasingly, do – from theology: one Josiah Church, about whom little seems to be known, inveighed in his 1648 pamphlet *The Divine Warrant of Infant-Baptism* against 'the *Quisquillian* toys of the Papists'.

It was too good a word to be limited to rants against Catholicism, of course, and the first secular use seems to be an excellent put-down by the writer and salonnière Hester Lynch Piozzi (aka Thrale), who was born on this day in 1741. 'There is however,' she wrote of one victim of her diarist's pen, 'something trifling in his Character, something *Quisquilian*.' A good word to have ready in case one meets another such person.

Lipoxeny

It is usually said that Benjamin Franklin, born on this day in 1706, was the first to observe that 'Fish, and guests, stink after three days,' though he himself attributed this phrasing to his father, and it is in turn a restatement of an older form of proverbial wisdom, viz. 'Fresh fish and new-come guests smell, but that they are three days old.' However you wish to put it, though, Franklin was certainly the kind of man with whom one can empathize in his desire to celebrate the moment of *lipoxeny*. This is Greek for 'leaving the host', and is used in botany for the phenomenon whereby certain fungal parasites desert, after a time, the plant they have been feeding on. So, too, one may be grateful for those *lipoxenous* types who finally leave the bar after cadging drinks all evening.

Ouphe

An elf or goblin, or the child of an elf or goblin, is an *ouphe*. In Shakespeare's *The Merry Wives of Windsor* – entered in the Stationers' Register for publication on this day in 1602 – Mistress Page happens upon the cunning plan of dressing her children and their friends 'like urchins, ouphes, and fairies' in order to alarm Falstaff. If you are elfin, meanwhile, you are also *ouphish* or *ouphant*.

The root is the Old Norse *alfr* meaning 'elf', from which is also derived *aufe* – strictly, only an elf's or goblin's child or a changeling left by the fairies, and so a misbegotten infant lacking normal intellectual powers (*OED*). This is how the later form of the word, *oaf*, which initially also meant 'changeling', acquired the more general sense of a stupid or dimwitted person, and became the kind of insult so delicately employed by such later geniuses as P. G. Wodehouse ('Would I be correct in describing him as a pumpkin-headed oaf?'). Thus often lurks beneath our everyday badinage a lost world of the supernatural.

19 January

Bafflegab

On this day in 1952, newspapers reported that a young American lawyer had received an award for inventing a new word. The man was Milton A. Smith, assistant at the US Chamber of Commerce, and his word was *bafflegab*. Formed quite simply from *baffle* and *gab*, to mean 'confusing talk', the word was meant to replace the unwieldy *gobbledygook* to refer to jargon-laden official communications – or, as Smith defined it: 'Multiloquence characterised by a consummate interfusion of circumlocution or periphrasis, inscrutability, incognizability, and other familiar manifestations of abstruse expatiation commonly utilised for promulgations implementing procrustean determinations by governmental bodies.'

Smith's early ideas for the coinage were *burobabble* and *gabbalia*, but he was probably right to choose *bafflegab*, which did enjoy a certain popularity over the next few decades, even if it never quite overtook *officialese*, which dates from as long ago as 1884. You might still prefer *bafflegab* as a straight-talking insult.

Izzard

The letter *z* was until not so long ago known as the *izzard*, first written as *ezod* in 1597 on a treatise on music by the English composer Thomas Morley. Morley is thought by some to have collaborated with Shakespeare, writing music for his plays: he certainly composed a setting of the song 'It was a Lover and his Lass' from *As You Like It*. No one knows for sure, though, whether that tune was indeed used at the play's first performance – possibly on this day in 1599 at Richmond Palace.

Coincidentally it was another composer, William Holden, who in his philological inquiry *Elements of Speech* (1669) went into rather spectacular detail on the last letter of the alphabet (as on all the others): '*Z* hath something peculiar,' he wrote, 'and in that it is accounted as a double letter (which it is not in the natural alphabet, any more than *S*), we may imagine it to have been anciently pronounced, as it is now by the Italians, *Ds* or *Ts*; and so to be called *zad* from the Hebrew *Tsade*; but yet to make out my observation, we, who pronounce it as a single letter, do so as often call it *yzard*.' Sadly, *izzard* is not recorded after 1837, but a resurrection of it could at least make spelling more fun.

Quidditative

Among philosophers, *quidditative* means having to do with the essence of a thing (from the philosophical sense of *quiddity*: see 26 June), but we are more interested in its other meaning: full of useless subtleties and equivocations. *Quidditative* – a silly word to describe a silly kind of pedantic argument – is first recorded in 1611 and defined as 'doubtful, obscure, full of quirks, fraught with quiddities'. (From 1539, a 'quiddity' was a quibble.)

It was employed energetically by the Scottish theologian George Gillespie, born on this day in 1613, who in his *A Dispute against the English Popish Ceremonies Obtruded upon the Church of Scotland* (1637) defended Scottish Presbyteranism against the attempted imposition of Catholic worship by Charles I. His theological adversaries were weak, intemperate, and *quidditative*, Gillespie fulminated. Such was the offence taken by the government, the Privy Council ordered all copies of the book to be returned and burnt, but some survived – and so, happily, does this word.

Lucubration

Those tireless souls who compose or study by night are adepts of the art of *lucubration*. From Latin *lux* ('light'), the verb to *lucubrate* literally means to work by means of artificial light, and so in Dr Johnson's day it was specifically 'study by candlelight'. Later, Lord Byron, born on this day in 1788, wrote in *Beppo*: 'I like to speak and *lucubrate* my fill.' No doubt with some self-irony; for *lucubrations* had by then acquired the extra meaning of overworked, unnecessarily elaborate pieces: ones that the author had been up all night polishing. But in a modern age where sleep is the pinnacle of an employee's productivity-enhancing strategies, perhaps *lucubration* is now a heroic counter-cultural practice.

Minacious

Something that is *minacious* is threatening, from the Latin *minae*, 'menaces'. (Whence also the less chewy synonym, *minatory*.) Over the history of its usage, a cold temperature and the authority of the law have been felt as *minacious*; as have individuals, or especially a gang of people. Sometimes, wrote the seventeenth-century philosopher Henry More, the heavens might look down on us with a 'sad and *minacious* countenance', and one still knows the feeling.

The jazz critic Gary Giddins, with impressive casualness, drops in this evocative word when writing that, on one session, a guitarist 'began his recording with a weirdly *minacious* intro that seemed to augur a train piece'. The musician in question was the legendary Django Reinhardt, born on this day in 1910.

Terriculament

A *terriculament* (from the Latin for 'small frightener') is something you are afraid of but needn't be, such as a moth, or a purely imaginary terror, such as a dragon or a *bugbear* (originally, a demon said to devour small children). Its earliest use, in 1548, speaks of 'vain *terriculaments* and rattlebladders'. (A *rattlebladder* was a kind of bladder-based rattle that was used to scare off birds.) Not irrelevantly to modern controversies, meanwhile, a *terriculament* can also be a kind of boo-word, or a term of threatened denunciation, as the bishop and writer Jeremy Taylor wrote in 1647: 'The name Heretic is made a *terriculamentum* to affright people from their belief.'

Ghost stories and horror fiction, of course, have long been the source of enduring *terriculaments* to those who encounter them at an impressionable age. One of the great inventors of such figures is the author of *The Sandman*, the German writer E. T. A. Hoffmann, who was born on this day in 1776.

Enantiodromia

From the Greek for 'opposite running', *enantiodromia* describes the curious process by which one thing becomes its opposite. In philosophy, this is applied to the thought of Heraclitus, who wrote: 'Cold things warm, warm things cool, wet things dry and parched things get wet' – in other words, one idea or state is always superseded by its contrary.

Closer to home and more usefully, perhaps, an *enantiodromia* also occurs when beliefs are inverted: when a community adopts the opposite view to that it formerly held, or when an individual changes his or her mind about something. As Carl Jung wrote, upon introducing the term to psychoanalysis: 'A good example of *enantiodromia* is seen in the psychology of Saul of Tarsus and his conversion to Christianity.' (Today is St Paul's Day, the feast of that conversion.) Less dramatically, having first refused a glass of wine, you may grandly announce having experienced an *enantiodromia*, while holding out your hand.

Apricity

To celebrate the gradual lengthening of the days after last month's winter solstice, we might unearth the beautiful word *apricity*, defined in Henry Cockeram's 1623 *The English Dictionary; or, An Interpreter of Hard English Words* as 'The warmness of the Sun in Winter'. This is so obscure that the *OED* has no other examples, but it is formed from the slightly more common verb *apricate*, which means either 'to bask in the sun' or 'to expose to sunlight' (from the Latin *apricus*, 'exposed to the sun').

The biographer John Aubrey says of Sir Thomas More, for example, that he liked to repair to the top of his little gatehouse: 'His Lordship was wont to recreate himself in this place to *apricate* and contemplate, and his little dog with him.' As Thomas De Quincey extended its sense, the light need not even be the sun's: he described someone poetically as 'Not sunning, but *mooning* himself – *apricating* himself in the occasional moonbeams'. For such pleasures it might still be best to wait till spring.

Festinate

To *festinate* (Latin *festinare*) is to make haste, but in a refined and delicate way, or to hurry something along. It appears adjectivally in *King Lear* (Cornwall: 'Advise the Duke where you are going, to a most festinate preparation'), and was a favourite word of Shelley, who observed in a letter of 1812 that 'It is possible to *festinate* or retard the progress of human perfectibility.'

The issue of *Punch* magazine published on this day in 1872 featured a satirical 'Diary of the Coming Woman', in which it is recorded that Hale Columbia Spragg, the first woman President of the United States, had visited London for a grand conference: 'Went to the Saloon, but it immediately adjourned, on the motion of Mr Theodore Stuke, to enable the Lady Members to *festinate* to the Congress.' The narrator also writes that she 'tunnelled over to Paris' for an afternoon's shopping, which was, after all, rather visionary.

28 January

Finifugal

Lionel Arthur Tollemache is described rather enviably by the *Oxford Dictionary of National Biography* as 'a writer and man of leisure': he is best remembered today for his collection of *Talks with Mr Gladstone* (1898), Tollemache having first met the future prime minister on this day in 1857. He also coined a word that deserves wider application: *finifugal*, or 'having a horror of endings'. In his book *Safe Studies* (1883), Tollemache mentions that another writer once told him that classical writers 'disliked the idea of sunset, and recoiled from the end of everything'. Whether or not that was true, he continued, such a '*finifugal* tendency, as we may call it', was noticeable in modern life too, especially in friends who 'have a morbid abhorrence of wishing one good-bye'. In our day, too, the *finifugal* tendency is everywhere, from those who hate to break off relationships, to some, one hears, who even put off finishing the books they are writing.

Callipygian

A person who is *callipygian* is one blessed with beautiful buttocks, for that is what the Greek means. The *Callipygian Venus* is a Roman marble statue of that goddess looking coyly back over her shoulder. The word is employed, meanwhile, by moralistic writers who use it as a synonym for disgusting luxuriousness, as well as by other writers for a classy-sounding thrill.

That, to be generous, is the sense in which it is employed in an English translation of a novel by the Spanish writer Vicente Blasco Ibáñez, who was born on this day in 1867 and would become most famous as the author of bullfighting epic *Blood and Sand*. In a less celebrated work, the erotic potboiler *Sónnica* (as translated in 1912 by Frances Douglas), we read of the following goings-on: 'The dancers, their feet together and limbs half opened, descended in a slow spiral, with gentle undulations, until they touched the floor; the instant their *callipygian* charms grazed the mosaic, they recoiled like suddenly awakened serpents, and the castanets clacked and the timbrel beat louder, accompanied by the howls of the musicians who animated them with lascivious words and exclamations of supreme abandon.'

30 January

Captation

A person always in the business of currying favours or applause is one employed in *captation*, from the Latin *captare*, 'seize' or 'grasp at'. Thomas Blount defines it as 'subtlety to get favour, a cunning endeavour to get a thing', and it has been applied in particular to the comportment of politicians over the centuries. The book known as the *Eikon Basilike* (Greek for 'royal portrait'), subtitled *The Portraiture of His Sacred Majesty in His Solitudes and Sufferings*, was purportedly written in the weeks before his execution by Charles I, who was put to death on this day in 1649. He, perhaps, had more reason than most to cast shade on civilian power-mongers in promising (if he indeed wrote the book) to make his case without any of the 'popular *captations*, which some men use in their Speeches'. In modern terms, indeed, we might define a 'populist' politician in particular as one who is all *captations* and little else.

Rambooze

If you ever wondered what students and fellows at the University of Cambridge were wont to drink in the seventeenth century, wonder no more: they quaffed *rambooze*. It is defined invitingly thus in 1656: '*Rambooz*, a compound drink, at Cambridge ... is commonly made of Eggs, Ale, Wine and Sugar; but in Summer, of Milk, Wine, Sugar, and Rose water.' The *OED* suggests it is formed from *booze* with an uncertain prefix (probably not *rum*), but notes too that *booze* by itself is not recorded till a century later. The actor Charles Dibdin, who was thrust into fame by his role in a musical drama, Isaac Bickerstaff's *The Maid of the Mill*, which premiered on this day in 1765, was also a prolific songwriter, and composed a fine paean to the drink: 'To be Jove, or Apollo, or Mars, would ye choose, / Ah! you've nothing to do but get drunk with *Rambooze*. / Then – a nat'ral transition – from heav'n if you go / Down to hell, ah! you'll find them all drinking below ...'

Even before that, one could refer to drink by the older term *bouse* (also *bowse*), which was also a verb for 'to drink, swill, or guzzle alcohol': its origin is unknown, but its first recorded use, in 1300, is an admiring paean to thirsty divines. 'Hail ye holy monkes ... deep can ye *bouse*.' Holy indeed.

FEBRUARY

Subtrist

On this day in 1587, Elizabeth I signed the death warrant of Mary, Queen of Scots, who was executed a week later. She had previously spent nineteen years in prison, one of them in Loch Leven Castle, and it is the time of that incarceration, and her subsequent escape, that Walter Scott chose as the milieu for his 1820 novel *The Abbot*. Therein we find a beautiful, melancholic word for a shade of mood. If you are just a little bit sad, you may be said to be *subtrist* (Latin *sub-*, 'under', and *tristus*, 'sad'). At one point Scott's hero Roland is greeted by a doctor thus: 'You are of the age when lads look after a bonny lass with one eye, and a dainty plum with another. But hey! You look *subtrist* and melancholic – I fear the maiden has proved cruel, or the plums unripe.'

Certainly to find one's plums unripe is no great cause for sobbing, but it might indeed make one *subtrist*.

Obganiate

There being no shortage of species of annoying person, we should renew terms that precisely define a particular kind of tedious vice, and *obganiate* is one of these: it means to irritate someone by repeating the same thing over and over. It comes from the Latin *obgannire*, 'to snarl or yelp like a dog', and a person who resembles such a yapping dog is guilty of the crime of *obganning*, seemingly interminable repetition.

Obganiate appears first in the seminal 1623 *English Dictionary* by Henry Cockeram, of whom we know very little save that he might have been the man of the same name who got married to one Elizabethe Strashley on this day in 1613. Leaving little other trace behind but his masterwork, he was definitely not an *obganiator*.

Ylem

What was the first stuff that existed? In early Big Bang theory, the primordial matter at the creation of the universe was christened *ylem*. This comes from the Greek *hyle*, meaning 'timber', used by philosophers to mean matter in general. It was unearthed by a team of scientists including the cosmologist Ralph Asher Alpher, born on this day in 1921, as well as George Gamow and Hans Bethe, who in a paper for the *Physical Review* in 1948 proposed the term in its new context: 'The word "ylem" is an obsolete noun meaning "The primordial substance from which the elements were formed". It seems highly desirable that a word of so appropriate a meaning be resurrected.'

Previously, the etymological equivalents *hyle* or *hyla* had been the preferred form of the word, but it turns out that the medieval poet John Gower, a friend of Chaucer's, had got there long before in his *Confessio Amantis* (1390), which refers to 'That matter universal, / Which hight [is called] *Ylem* in special'.

Cacotechny

From the Greek words for 'evil' and 'art', *cacotechny* was first defined in John Ash's 1775 *New Dictionary* as 'a hurtful invention', since when many more hurtful inventions have been invented. In the nineteenth century it is defined as both 'a corrupt art' and 'a depraved style of art', so that it was possible to use it to describe the daubings of a terrible painter as well as a noxious innovation. In our day, however, the suffix *–techny* will inevitably invoke *technology* (literally, 'the study of arts or crafts'), and our age, like all the others, has also seen its fair share of *cacotechny*.

The website Facebook was founded on this day in 2004.

Pejorist

If you think the world is getting worse and worse, you are a *pejorist*, but this is not quite the same as being an out-and-out doom-monger. At least according to the poet and scholar A. E. Housman, who wrote in a letter on this day in 1933: 'I have never had any such thing as a "crisis of pessimism". In the first place, I am not a pessimist but a *pejorist* (as George Eliot said she was not an optimist but a meliorist); and that philosophy is based on my observation of the world, not on anything so trivial and irrelevant as personal history.'

For George Eliot, an optimist believed that the world would get better by itself, but a *meliorist* (from the Latin for 'better') believed that it could only be improved through human effort. So, for Housman, a *pejorist* (Latin for 'worse') believes that the world is being made worse through concentrated human effort. And he didn't even know about global warming.

Puckeroo

Today is Waitangi Day in New Zealand, commemorating the founding treaty of the nation signed in 1840. It is a fine reason to publicize the word *puckeroo*, derived from the Maori *pakaru*, which the *OED* defines as 'useless, broken, out of order; destroyed, finished', and so is one of those highly satisfying words you will almost certainly have occasion to use on a daily basis.

It is also possible to say something is *puckarooed*, as in Sally T. Ollivier's 1965 novel glorying in the title *Petticoat Farm*. 'I come to see if you've got a spare shovel,' one character says to another. 'Mine's puckarooed and I got a cow in the drain.' Aren't we all, in a very real sense, in that exact situation?

Nemesism

Born on this day in 1907, the psychologist Saul Rozenzweig coined the surprisingly underused term *nemesism* for a sort of relentless self-criticism or hostility. 'The psycho-analyst,' he wrote in 1938, 'might appropriately call the turning of aggression upon the individual's own self "*nemesism*" from the name of the Greek goddess of vengeance.' That goddess, of course, is Nemesis, winged punisher of *hubris*, or overweening ambitious pride. Rozenzweig intended *nemesism* explicitly to be the opposite syndrome to that we still identify far more often, *narcissism*, Narcissus being the beautiful man who fell in love with his own reflection. No doubt there are many narcissists around, but there must also be many *nemesisists*, suffering quietly.

Irrefragable

What is *irrefragable* cannot be denied – or, as Samuel Johnson put it, is 'Not to be confuted; superior to argumental opposition'. It comes from the Latin for 'unopposable', and has been applied both to arguments and to people. The art critic John Ruskin, who was born on this day in 1819, vouchsafes in his *Modern Painters* (1846) that he considers the early Italian masters to be 'in all points of principle (not, observe, of knowledge or empirical attainment) ... the most *irrefragable* authorities, precisely on account of the child–like innocence' of their art.

It is perhaps an article of modern faith (or the lack of it) that nothing is *irrefragable* in this sense, but the term has also been used to mean 'obstinate' (i.e. unwilling to be opposed), as when Robert Burton laments the stubbornness of young people nowadays in *The Anatomy of Melancholy*. Young women, he complains 'think no body good enough for them', while 'Many young men are as obstinate, and as curious in their choice, as *irrefragable* and peevish on the other side.'

Zamzawed

Few are the cooks who have not suddenly remembered leaving a dish in the oven, only to find it now *zamzawed* beyond all saving. This exotic-looking word is actually the Devonshire dialect version of *sam-sodden*, which means 'half-done' or 'half-baked' (in metaphorical as well as literal terms), but somehow its meaning became inverted, so that *zamzawed* usually means *too* well done, ruined by excessive cooking.

The writer Mary Palmer, who was born on this day in 1716, became famous for her *Devonshire Dialogue*, a samizdat compendium (published only posthumously) of descriptions of Devonshire custom. In it, one poor man finds that 'His meat was *zam-zaw'd* and a bowl'd to jouds [rags]'. One could as well use it today as as a more vivid synonym for *overdone*, applied to artistic productions as well as to food.

Desuetude

Not quite itself having fallen into desuetude, the word *des-uetude* (pronounced dessʏouɪtude) is still available to mean 'the state of no longer being used'. From the Latin for 'to become unaccustomed', it can mean either (formerly) the abandonment of a practice or study, or (now most commonly) the state of abandon that thing now finds itself in: the limbo of disuse.

The essayist Charles Lamb observed sadly in 1823 that birthdays were no longer the profound occasions for reflection on one's mortality that they once (supposedly) were. 'In the gradual *desuetude* of old observances,' he wrote, 'this custom of solemnizing our proper birth-day hath nearly passed away, or is left to children, who reflect nothing at all about the matter, nor understand anything in it beyond cake and orange.' Let us therefore, with all due solemnity, celebrate the birth of Lamb himself, on this day in 1775.

Diallelus

Lines that are *diallel* are distinguished from lines that are *parallel* because the former cross. A mathematical pedant will note that every pair of non-parallel lines will cross somewhere, thus rendering the term *diallel* somewhat redundant. It has persisted in biology, though, for a programme of breeding that produces every possible cross-breed. It was first used in this sense by the Danish biologist Johannes Schmidt, in a 1919 paper entitled 'Racial Studies in Fishes', which explained the method thus: 'With a number of trout I perform what I have called *diallel* crossings. It consists in this that *each female is paired with each male*.' Unlike many experimental animals, at least those fish were having a good time.

The related phenomenon of *diallelus* comes from the same Greek root, meaning 'through or by means of one another', but in this case it refers to circular reasoning: the attempt to establish one idea by appeal to another, and vice versa simultaneously. Some philosophers say that, because every idea depends for support on something else, our whole system of thought might be one great *diallelus*. To refute such corrosive scepticism was one of the primary aims, if not one now widely accepted as successful, of the philosopher René Descartes, who died on this day in 1650.

Apodeictic

What is *apodeictic* is incontrovertible, subject to definitive evidence or absolute proof. Eventually from the Greek *deiknon*, 'to show', it is sometimes also written *apodictic*, as Thomas Blount's *Glossographia* has it: '*Apodictical* (from *apodixis*) pertaining to a plain proof, or demonstration of a thing.'

Later, Coleridge spoke of the certainties available in the art of geometry, where 'there exist truths of *apodictic* force in Reason, which the mere Understanding strives in vain to comprehend'. The philosopher Immanuel Kant, who died on this day in 1804, similarly used *apodictic* for necessary truths that could be known purely by reasoning, without any recourse to experience, such as those in mathematics. But perhaps it can do service in the modern age as a stronger, more insistent word for what is firmly established, even if everywhere doubted.

13 February

Cacoethes

Catherine Howard was beheaded on this day in 1542, a victim of Henry VIII's notoriously inexhaustible *cacoethes* (pronounced kakoᴇᴛʜᴇs), an urge to do something bad. It comes from the Greek *kakos* ('evil', hence *cacophony*, 'bad sound', and so forth) and *ethos* ('character'). The story 'The Last of the Lairds', published in *Fraser's Magazine* in 1836 and attributed to one Candidus, remarks: 'There is a *cacoëthes* in many of us so strong – in some of scribbling, in some of building, and in others, again, of painting – that to prevent its exercise were as hopeless a task as that of stemming the mountain torrent, or sailing up the cataract of Niagara.' True enough, but the laird of the story was doubly vexed, for he had a double *cacoethes*: 'One half of it was a *cacoëthes* of building, the other half *cacoëthes* of planting. Both combined would merge in the word *furor.*' You can imagine the pressure on the laird's fortunes caused by his irrepressible urge to put trees and crazily designed enormous houses in the most inauspicious places.

Long ago, the Roman poet Juvenal famously wrote of *insanabile scribendi cacoethes*, 'the insane desire to write', something that has been, and remains, an affliction for very many unfortunate persons.

14 FEBRUARY

Cataglottism

St Valentine was supposedly martyred on this day in 269 CE, and during the Middle Ages his feast day began to be associated with romantic love, it being thought that birds also paired around this time of year. Surprisingly, perhaps, birds also practise *cataglottism*, or kissing with the tongue (from the Greek for 'use of the tongue into', as *polyglottism* is 'having several tongues'). As the British doctor and sexologist Havelock Ellis wrote in his *Studies in the Psychology of Sex* (1897): 'Many animals rub or lick each other. The mucous surfaces share in this irritability of the skin. The kiss is not only an expression of feeling; it is a means of provoking it. *Cataglottism* is by no means confined to pigeons.' By no means.

Supervacaneousness

One might like to think that Dr Johnson was chuckling to himself when he included this word in his *Dictionary*, with the single-word definition 'Needlessness'. Is it not, after all, itself rather a needless word? Well, too far down that path and we shall have no synonyms or poetry. Besides, *supervacaneous* is rather a beautiful adjective, formed from the Latin *super* ('above'), plus *vacare*, 'to be empty or void'. So it denotes something not just empty but *super*-empty, a really utterly futile and redundant thing.

A piquant instance of the word occurs in philosopher Jeremy Bentham's 1825 broadside against Lord Eldon's failures to reform the courts. Eldon had insisted he was 'uncorrupted in office' and hoped his successor would have 'an equal desire to execute his duties with fidelity'. To which Bentham – born on this day in 1748 – responded sarcastically: '*Desire!* And so, in an office such as that of Chief-Judge … *desire* is sufficient: *accomplishment*, or anything like an approach to it, supervacaneous!'

Zetetic

Inquiring minds deserve the name *zetetic*, which means 'investigating or proceeding by inquiry', from the Greek *zetein*, 'to seek'. Curiously, in the nineteenth century, 'zetetic astronomers' were Flat Earthers, after an 1849 pamphlet entitled *Zetetic Astronomy: A description of several experiments which prove that the surface of the sea is a perfect plane and that the Earth is not a Globe!* More usually, however, *zetetic* has described those who avoid all proud dogmatism, and was sometimes used interchangeably with 'sceptic', as a writer in 1895 referred to 'Sceptics and Zetetics, indicat[ing] that they were always in search of truth without flattering themselves that they had found it'.

The novelist Iain Banks was born on this day in 1954; in his 1996 science-fiction novel *Excession*, we read of a splendid offshoot of the enlightened Culture civilization that glories in the name of the *Zetetic Elench*. The root of 'Elench' is the Greek *elenchos*, 'cross-examination', often used of Socrates's questioning method. So, happily, the Zetetic Elench were questioning inquirers.

Auscultation

The French doctor René Laënnec was born on this day in 1781, and in 1816 he made a great discovery. Presented in hospital with a young woman suffering from symptoms of heart disease, he felt unable for reasons of modesty to put his ear to the patient's chest. So instead he rolled some sheets of paper into a cylinder and listened through that, discovering to his surprise that he could hear the heartbeat much more distinctly. Refining his idea over the next three years, he invented the first *stethoscope*, made from a hollow tube of wood, naming it after the Greek for 'chest examination'.

In 1819, Laënnec published the results of his research, *De l'Auscultation Médiate*, or *On Mediated Auscultation*. The word *auscultation* is a general word for 'listening', particularly 'hearkening or paying close attention to what is heard', and the stethoscope allowed for mediated rather than direct *auscultation* (putting the ear to the chest), which amplified the sound. Later, Sir Henry Taylor's essay *The Statesman* (1836) observes: 'He who can listen with real attention to every thing that is said to him, has a great gift of *auscultation*.' It is a gift still worth prizing.

Postriduan

What is *postriduan* relates to the following day; so, for example, having enjoyed a night of carousing, you might then want some *postriduan* eggs and coffee. It comes simply from the Latin for '(on a) later day', and seems useful enough to employ proverbially: never do today what can be rendered *postriduan*.

It is claimed in a sixteenth-century manual of 'occult philosophy' that 'all *Postriduan* days are called black days', which is confusing since the author seems at the same time to be saying that black days are the anniversaries of notable catastrophes – such as the Romans' defeat by Hannibal at the Battle of Canae – rather than the days after. Perhaps only adepts were meant to understand this as written: the author was the famous German physician, soldier, and black magician Heinrich Cornelius Agrippa, who died (or did he?) on this day in 1535.

Solander

A box that opens like a book – in which you might store letters, photographs, file records, or other things – is called a *solander*. Pleasingly, this is an eponym, a word adopted in honour of a specific person, for it was the Swedish natur- alist Daniel Carlsson Solander – born on this day in 1733 – who invented this type of box while he was cataloguing the collection of the Natural History Museum in London.

What's more, Solander and the English naturalist Joseph Banks were the two scientists accompanying Captain James Cook aboard HMS *Endeavour* on his voyage to Australia and New Zealand (1768–71), and their presence is why there is to this day a Botany Bay in Sydney. It is also why the poet William Cowper could say, as the first recorded use of the word in a 1788 letter to a friend: 'I shall be as happy in the arrival of my *Solander* as he whose name it bears was to arrive once more in England after his circumnavigation.'

Sarcast

Someone gifted in the arts of sarcasm may be called a *sarcast*, a word with a pleasingly biting sound – which is appropriate, since the Greek root of both words means to tear flesh or gnash the teeth. Some writers have equated the *sarcast* with the cynic, which seems unfair; for the cynic, properly speaking, believes in nothing at all, while the sarcast employs her wit in defence of values she sees neglected.

Benjamin Disraeli, who became prime minister for the second time on this day in 1874, was called by his rival William Gladstone 'a great sarcast', which some would not mind having for an epitaph.

Deisal

W. H. Auden, born on this day in 1907, loved an archaic word now and again; in his long poem *The Age of Anxiety* (which, anxious reader, it was already in 1947), he harks back to the 'Primal Age / When we danced deisal'. *Deisal* comes from the Gaelic *deiseil* (ultimately from the Latin *dexter*) meaning 'towards the right', and describes rightward or clockwise motion. For the ancient Celts it brought good luck to process in such a manner, following the apparent course of the sun: such a form of worship was still attested in parts of Scotland, where an eighteenth-century observer wrote of a parish where, to celebrate marriages and baptisms, 'they make a procession round the church, *Deasoil*, i.e., sunways'.

Somewhat more satirically, Sir Walter Scott in *Waverley* (1814) describes a Highland surgeon who refuses to attend to our hero 'until he had perambulated his couch three times, moving from east to west, according to the course of the sun. This, which was called making the *deasil*, both the leech and the assistants seemed to consider as a matter of the last importance to the accomplishment of a cure.' There is still no shortage of such superstitions in the finer sorts of quackery.

Quidnunc

Quidnunc is Latin for 'What now?', and so a person who continually asks such questions is called a *quidnunc*: an inveterate gossip, or an annoyingly pestering and inquisitive person. Sir Leslie Stephen, writer and founding editor of the *Dictionary of National Biography*, who died on this day in 1904, offers this agreeably waspish portrait of the eighteenth-century politician and writer Horace Walpole: 'For many years, Walpole's greatest pleasure seems to have been drinking tea with Lady Suffolk, and carefully piecing together bits of scandal about the courts of the first two Georges. He tells us, with all the brilliance of a philosopher describing a brilliant scientific induction, how he was sometimes able, by adding bits of gossip to hers, to unravel the secret of some wretched intrigue which had puzzled two generations of *quidnuncs*.'

The *quidnuncs* are still at large, of course, and such an addiction to enjoyable gossip, termed *quidnuncism*, is a syndrome doubtless eternal in human nature.

Amate

John Keats, who died on this day in 1821, composed an elegy for an earlier tragic poet, Thomas Chatterton, who had taken his own life at the age of seventeen. 'Oh! How nigh / Was night to thy fair morning,' go the lines. 'Thou didst die / A half-blown flow'ret which cold blasts *amate*.' *Amate*, attested since 1320, means to daunt, overwhelm, or dismay, from the old French *mat*, 'dejected'.

If you are so dismayed or downcast, you can still say that you are *amated*, though *amate* itself can also be used adjectivally: in John Lydgate's 1430 verse retelling of the Trojan War (known as *Troy Book*), the Trojan prince Troilus is described standing 'Of long fighting awhaped [stupefied] and *amate*, / And from his folks alone desolate'. Immediately after this, the furious Achilles smites off Troilus's head, which perhaps was a mercy.

Absonous

The Latin *absonus* means 'unpleasant-sounding', 'discordant', or 'tasteless', and so it was imported into English in 1622, when a noise was said to be 'either sweet and melodious, or harsh and *absonous*'. It could enjoy wider use today, however, in its secondary meaning, which Dr Johnson gives as 'absurd, contrary to reason'. Such is one way of describing the existentially surreal drama of the French stage in the mid-twentieth century, such as Eugène Ionesco's *Rhinocéros* (1959; see 4 May); it was the English scholar Martin Esslin, who died on this day in 2002, who coined for it the term 'theatre of the absurd'.

A writer for the *Lancet* observed meanwhile in 1828: 'Medical science . . . can no longer be impeded by the *absonous* and ridiculous dogmas of less auspicious times.' When the global age of sweet reason dawns, we might have no more use for it, but till then *absonous* will be quite handy.

Anacamptic

What would you expect to hear in an *anacamptic* space? Well, the word comes from the Greek for 'to turn back'. So, as a 1706 dictionary defines it: '*Anacamptical* or *Anacamptick*, Reflecting, Turning or Bowing back or again, a Word often used with respect to Echoes, which are Sounds produced *Anacamptically* or by Reflection.' The Royal Festival Hall in London was one of the first concert halls to be built with the principles of scientific acoustics in mind: there, on this day in 2004, Brian Wilson brought to a close his run of performances of his lost album, *Smile*. The cheers echoed *anacamptically* to the rafters.

Such turning-back can also happen, of course, to light, and so the plural *anacamptics* was used in the eighteenth century to mean the science of optical reflection (later called *catoptrics*, from the Greek for a mirror) as well as of acoustic echoes. Much reflection ensued.

Fugle

Thomas D'Urfey, who died on this day in 1723, was an English playwright, poet, and comic writer, who between 1719 and 1720 published a mammoth six-volume work entitled *Wit and Mirth; or, Pills to Purge Melancholy*, the title of which itself might in some cantankerous breasts be sufficient to provoke melancholy. Nonetheless, it is this belly-clutching compendium that is credited with the first printed use of the verb *fugle*, which means to trick or cheat, though dictionaries do not know why. A later sense of *fugle* meaning to guide or direct is a back-formation from the military *fugleman*, from the German *flügelmann*, for the leader of the file. But D'Urfey's use of the earlier sense is evidently unrelated to this meaning, occurring as it does in a song entitled 'The Yeoman of Kent', which goes: 'In *Kent* I hear, there lately did dwell / Long *George*, a *Yeoman* by trade, / Plump, lively and young, brisk, jolly and strong, / Who *fugell'd* the Parson's fine Maid.' You can see what he did there, can't you?

Palinode

Rather than submit to charges of having made a 'U-turn' or a 'climbdown', politicians who wish to ennoble the fact of having changed their minds could announce that they were executing a *palinode*. This is a recantation or withdrawal of a sentiment; in Scottish law it also meant a formal recantation demanded of someone found guilty of defamation. The word comes from the Greek for 'song' and 'over again', and originally meant specifically a song or poem in which the author denies or retracts a sentiment made in an earlier work. The ur-example is that of Stesichorus, the Greek lyric poet of the seventh century BCE, said to have been magically blinded for composing verses that Helen of Troy found insulting. Adroitly, he then composed his *palinode*, recanting his earlier verses and stating that Helen bore no responsibility at all for the Trojan War; his sight was restored.

In the modern age, perhaps the most magnificent palinode is that executed by Leonard Nimoy, who died on this day in 2015. In 1975, fed up with being seen only as a *Star Trek* character, he published an autobiography entitled *I Am Not Spock*. Twenty years later, with majestic aplomb, he published a palinodic second volume: *I Am Spock*.

28 February

Acherontic

What is dark or hellish may be sonorously termed *acherontic*. In Greek mythology, Acheron was one of the rivers of Hades, the River of Woe: once you had crossed it, there was no going back. Sometimes it was used as a name for the whole Underworld itself, and hence the importation into English to mean something diabolical. In Thomas Middleton's religious poem *The Wisdom of Solomon Paraphras'd* (1597), he speaks of 'gloomy darkness, sin's eternal debtor . . . poisoned buds, from *Acharontick* stalk'. His fellow playwright Cyril Tourneur, who died on this day in 1626, writes likewise, in his early and not-much-loved allegorical poem *The Transformed Metamorphosis* (1600), of an Apollonian robe designed to protect the wearer from '*Acherontick* mists' on Earth.

Since then *acherontic* has been available to mean 'infernal' or 'extremely gloomy'. A nineteenth-century writer even complained of 'the demon hooting' of owls in 'these *Acherontic* woods', which seems rather a slander upon the owls.

Supererogatory

What is *supererogatory* is, according to the Latin derivation, something that goes beyond what is asked for, and is therefore unnecessary. In the preface to *Prometheus Unbound* (1820), Shelley writes: 'Didactic poetry is my abhorrence; nothing can be equally well expressed in prose that is not tedious and *supererogatory* in verse.' For three out of every four years, meanwhile, the 29th of February itself is *supererogatory*, and so the rest of this entry may safely be skipped.

Supererogatory, of course, means more or less the same as *supervacaneous* (see 15 February) — in which case, you might think, one of them is. But then, so are *superfluent*, *exsuperant*, *orra*, *traboccant*, and so forth. That there should be a *nimiety* (see 2 June) of such terms is, after all, quite fitting.

March

1 MARCH

Hwyl

Today is the feast of St David, patron saint of Wales, a nation that among an impressive roster of writers, actors, and musicians has also given the rest of the world the word *hwyl*. It is first recorded in English print in 1899, where it is defined as a form of emotive eloquence 'which seems to exert remarkable influence on the hearers', but it is more widely used in modern times to convey a sense of passion and belonging.

According to the historical dictionary of Welsh, *Geiriadur Prifysgol Cymru*, *hywl* originally meant the sail of a ship, and then acquired the sense of progress or a journey, from where it could signify the course of a life, and thence to a variety of uses including 'healthy physical or mental condition', an instrument's being in tune, 'fervour (esp. religious), ecstasy, unction, gusto, zest', and 'merry-making, hilarity, jollity, mirth, gaiety'. Nearly all of which senses are contained in the gloss on the word by rugby player Gavin Henson in 2006: '*Hwyl* is all about passion, spirit, and a sense of achievement – it really is how I felt after our win over the English.'

Charientism

If one wishes to soften the blow of hard news with a pleasantly light-hearted euphemism, one should employ *charientism*: according to Thomas Blount, 'a trope or manner of speaking which mitigates hard matters with pleasant words'. *Charientismos* (Greek) is variously defined as 'gracefulness of expression' or 'urbane irony'. As an example, the Roman rhetorician Quintilian offers the remark made by Themistocles when persuading the Athenians to abandon their city in order to man the ships against the Spartans. Instead of saying they needed to leave Athens undefended, he urged them to 'commit her to the protection of heaven'.

The English schoolmaster and writer John Clarke, who was buried on this day in 1658, explained in his Latin textbook *Phraseologia puerilis* (1638) that *charientism* differs from sarcasm in that, in using the former, I mean you no harm. Perhaps we all need a little to get through the day.

Collogue

If you wish to have a confidential meeting with someone, you may request a *collogue*, according to the 1887 supplement to the *Etymological Dictionary of the Scottish Language* compiled by Revd Dr John Jamieson, who was born on this day in 1759. The word, however, has rather a baffling history as a verb, for when first recorded, in 1602, to *collogue* means to employ blandishments or flattery with someone, and so 'flatter and collogue' becomes a common combination. By the middle of the seventeenth century, however, to collogue had acquired the meaning of 'to conspire or collude in secret', and this sense persisted.

In George Eliot's *Silas Marner* (1861), the Squire exclaims to his son Godfrey: 'And how long have you been so thick with Dunsey that you must *collogue* with him to embezzle my money?' At the same time, Thackeray, in *The Adventures of Philip* (1862), writes of old men who 'wagged their old heads sadly when they collogued in clubs', so to speak of *colloguing* is not necessarily to imply that there is malice afoot.

Malapert

D. H. Lawrence was buried on this day in 1930, having written many books considered *malapert* for the time. In his last play, *David* (1926), the biblical hero (and author's namesake) says: 'My brothers say of me, I am a cocksure *malapert*.' Since the fifteenth century, someone who is *malapert* is saucy or impudent. It seems to come from *mal*, 'badly', and *apert*, 'outspoken': so someone who is *malapert* is forward in the wrong way.

Not surprisingly, the word has often been used to police women's behaviour especially, as well as sundry 'malapert Clowns' (1738) and the odd 'malapert friar' (1638). It is nicer, perhaps, to use the word with grudging affection: according to Chaucer, Criseyde loved Troilus even though he was *malapert*.

Meldrop

On this day in 1824, Elisha Harris was born: he became the first president of the American Public Health Association, and was a pioneer of public sanitation and hygiene, with the aim of reducing outbreaks of infectious disease such as influenza. Should you nonetheless catch flu, or just a winter cold, you might soon have a *meldrop*, a very old word for 'a drop of mucus hanging or falling from a person's nose'. The term originally meant the foam from a horse's mouth, since a *mel* was a horse's bit in Old Icelandic. The fifteenth-century Scots poet Robert Henryson provides an early example, describing the god Saturn as grotesquely off-putting in appearance, one example of which is the fact that 'Out of his nose the meldrop fast can run.' Poor Saturn.

More prettily, a meldrop can also be water found in natural places, such as hanging off the end of leaves, or 'the drop at the end of an icicle, and indeed every drop in a pendent state', as defined in the *Etymological Dictionary of the Scottish Language* (1825).

Pickthank

What kind of a person is a *pickthank*? Someone who steals gratitude by devious means? Indeed: and so an informer, a flatterer, or sycophant. Its adjectival form can play a satisfying role in an eruption of bile, as in this marvellous line from the 1741 comedy *The Perjur'd Devotee: Or, The Force of Love* by Daniel Bellamy: 'I'll make thee an Example to all the politick, pimping, *pick-thank* Rogues in the Kingdom, you Dog, you.' Quite.

On this day in 1600, meanwhile, Shakespeare's *Henry IV, Part 1* was acted at court for the entertainment of the Flemish ambassador. In it, Prince Hal begs the King not to believe the words of 'smiling *pickthanks* and base news-mongers': two sorts of person, it must be noted, who remain much with us today.

Chronotope

Think about the road in a road movie, or the haunted house in a horror film. You are, perhaps, thinking about the *chronotope*, a term coined by the Russian literary theorist Mikhail Bakhtin, who died on this day in 1975. His original Russian word, хронотоп, as well as the direct English equivalent rendered by his translator, Caryl Emerson, is built from the Greek for 'time' and 'place' or 'space', and for Bakhtin is necessary to name the way time and space are framed together in narrative art. In his essay introducing the idea, he namechecks Einstein's sibling concept of spacetime, and says he is using a similar idea to express the 'inseparability of space and time' in literature.

'In the literary artistic *chronotope*,' Bakhtin continues, 'spatial and temporal indicators are fused into one carefully thought-out, concrete whole. Time, as it were, thickens, takes on flesh, becomes artistically visible; likewise, space becomes charged and responsive to the movements of time, plot and history.' This is a fruitful way to think about the spaceship USCSS *Nostromo* in the film *Alien* (1979), as well as the terrifyingly irrational house in Mark Z. Danielewski's novel *House of Leaves* (2000), which dramatizes just what can happen when the *chronotope* goes awry.

Epeolatry

In a celebrated 1919 decision, *Schenck vs United States*, Supreme Court Justice Oliver Wendell Holmes, Jr., who was born on this day in 1841, declared that free speech could not be absolute. Considering the matter of a man who had distributed leaflets opposing America's involvement in the First World War, Holmes wrote that the First Amendment could not protect words if they presented 'a clear and present danger that they will bring about the substantive evils that Congress has a right to prevent'.

In so deciding, Holmes resisted the lure of *epeolatry*, or the uncritical worship of words. This term had been coined by his father, the physician and poet Oliver Wendell Holmes Sr. in his 1859 essay collection, *The Professor at the Breakfast Table*. New translations of the Bible, he argued, rejuvenated ideas made dull by old language. 'Time, time only,' he wrote, 'can gradually wean us from our *Epeolatry*, or word-worship, by spiritualizing our ideas of the thing signified.'

Epeolatry (from the Greek *epeos*, 'word') is thus coined on the model of *idolatry* — it means something bad. Later writers agreed, with one newspaper observing in 1928: 'Many writers suffer from this disease of *epeolatry*, or word-worship.' Perhaps it is a kind of Stockholm syndrome.

Patzer

On this day in 1943, Bobby Fischer was born, and a mere fifteen years later he had become the youngest ever US chess champion. Interviewed at the age of eighteen, he was increasingly confident of his abilities, saying: 'When I meet those Russian *patzers* I'll put them in their place.' *Patzer* is not exactly a compliment, being chess slang for a bad player: it is a straight borrowing from the nineteenth-century German *Patzer*, meaning 'an incorrigible bungler'.

To be fair to Fischer, he did eventually steamroll the Russians and become World Champion himself. In the meantime, *patzer* is such a fine and satisfying word that it would be a shame to limit its use to the sixty-four squares of the chessboard. Are we not all surrounded by *patzers* every day?

Obelus

The division symbol ($\div$) is a mark with a longer and more dubious history than you might suspect, being also long known as the *obelus*. This comes straight from the Greek *obelos*, which meant (1) a pointed rod or nail, but also (2) a large pillar (whence *obelisk*), and further (3) a critical mark on a manuscript to signal doubtfulness or falsity. This critical mark usually took the form of a horizontal line (symbolizing the nail, or perhaps an arrow), sometimes with an asterisk, and sometimes with one point above the line and one below it: $\div$.

Because the *obelus* was often used to indicate that the marked text should be removed, it later seemed logical to appropriate it for the mathematical operation of division. The first person to do so was the Swiss mathematician Johann Rahn – born on this day in 1622 – in his 1659 work *Teutsche Algebra*. Since when, every schoolchild has known how to draw an *obelus*.

11 March

Ostentate

To show off is to *ostentate*, which is a more show-offy word, and so apt to the thing described. The Latin *ostentare* means 'to show off', or 'display too frequently', and thence too we have the more common noun *ostentation*. Martin Fotherby, theologian and Bishop of Salisbury, who died on this day in 1620, uses the verb in scholarly self-defence in his post-humously published *Atheomastix: Clearing Four Truths, Against Atheists and Infidels*: 'The citing of mine Authors so particularly ... was not to *ostentate*, and make shew of mine own reading.' Of course not; and neither is it ever so in our age either.

Insulse

Insulse is a fine old word for 'lacking wit or sense' (*OED*), or, more frankly, 'stupid'. The Irish philosopher George Berkeley (aka Bishop Berkeley) – born on this day in 1685 – uses it in his dialogue *Alciphron, or The Minute Philosopher* (1732), which is an attack on atheist free-thinkers. 'In our times a dull man is said to be insipid or *insulse*,' he writes, because among the ancients, 'salt was another name for wit.'

Indeed, as Latin *salsus* meant 'witty' or, literally, 'salted', so *insulse* means 'without wit'. (*Insipid*, meanwhile, means 'without taste'.) There being no lack of cause to complain of the dullness of others, we may increase the general merriment by revivifying the word *insulse*.

Collet

The front of a person's neck, the throat, was once delicately called the *collet*, being the French diminutive form of *col*, or 'neck'. *Collet* then could describe a garment's collar or a band or collar worn around the neck. (And so *décolleté* is a style that removes the collar or further exposes the throat.) From then its use widened further to include a metal ring or socket, part of a cannon, the place where a plant's roots join the stem, and the setting for a precious stone.

It is in this last sense that the word is used by John Boyle, Earl of Orrery, in his *Remarks on the Life and Writings of Dr. Jonathan Swift* (1751). Boyle was a friend of Swift's, but this book, which appeared after the great man's death, has been called a 'Judas-biography'. In it he speculates on whether Swift and the woman he called 'Stella' got married in secret. Wrote Boyle, pompously: 'A great genius must tread in unbeaten paths, and deviate from the common road of life: otherwise, surely a diamond of so much lustre [Stella] might have been publicly produced, although it had been fixed within the *collet* of matrimony.' The sparkling 'Stella' was actually named Esther Johnson, and she was born on this day in 1681.

Gowpen

If you hold out both your hands cupped together so that I might pour in a quantity of confectionery or other edibles, you are making a *gowpen*; and the amount that can fit in it is also a *gowpen*. It is gratifying to know that there is a word for such a human measure – effectively, a double handful – and a very old one: it comes from the Old Norse *gaupn*, whence also the alternative *yepsen*, which means the same thing. One of the Scots songs by eighteenth-century poet Allan Ramsay goes: 'When we came to London Town / We dream'd of gowd in *gowpings* here'; a later poet expresses the wealth of a lord by saying he has 'guineas in *gowpins*'.

The word is recorded as late as 1893 – '*Gowpen*, the hollow of both hands placed together' – in the two-volume dictionary of *Northumberland Words* compiled by the song-writer and historian Richard Oliver Heslop, who was born on this day in 1842. But as long as human beings have hands, and want things put in them, it should surely prove useful.

15 March

Naturesse

The soldier-prince John of Gaunt, a close friend of Geoffrey Chaucer's, was buried on this day in 1399. He was among a group of aristocratic thinkers who popularized the ethical concept of lordly benevolence, or what was called *naturesse*, from the French for 'naturalness'. The authorities at the University of Oxford wrote a letter in 1439 thanking the Duke of Gloucester for his '*naturesses* and benevolence' in donating money to the institution.

As a word for generosity, *naturesse* persisted for another century, and then gradually fell into disuse. This is a shame, since the idea that to be kind was the *natural* thing seems as radical now as it did then.

Horripilation

On this day in 1974, *The Exorcist* opened in British cinemas, following its American release on Boxing Day 1973, when it had been greeted by critics as 'sickening' and 'hateful'. Audiences on both sides of the Atlantic, though, flocked to see the film, and no doubt experienced some measure of *horripilation* at the events portrayed.

This is the technical term for 'flesh-creeping', coming from the Latin for something that causes the hair to bristle (i.e. stand up on end). Medical writers through the centuries have attributed *horripilation* to internal disease or cold conditions, but though it has nothing to do with the word *horror*, it seems a particularly apt word for the pleasurably unpleasant sensation that the finest works in that genre can produce.

Amain

On this day in 1743, the Reverend John Wesley, founder of Methodism, gave a sermon at the mining village of Pelton. 'One of the old colliers,' he later wrote, 'not much accustomed to things of this kind, in the middle of the sermon, began shouting *amain* for mere satisfaction and joy of heart. But their usual token of approbation (which somewhat surprised me at first) was clapping me on the back.'

Amain is a grand old word that means 'with full force', 'at full pelt', or 'immediately'. It comes from the Old English *mægn*, meaning 'power' – as does *main* itself, which first meant 'strong' before it acquired its modern sense of 'principal'. So Longfellow's 'The Wreck of the Hesperus' (1841): 'Down came the storm, and smote *amain* the vessel.' And so the English poet George Turberville in 1587: 'Who so doth run a race / Shall surely sweat *amain*, / And who so loves, shall hardly gloze / Of [be able to palliate, or gloss over] secret hidden pain.'

Punctilio

A *punctilio* (from the Italian *puntiglio*, 'small point') is a tiny detail of behaviour or argument: either, as various users have implied, a valuable nicety, or a hair-splitting diversion. Dr Johnson, for one, is positive: 'A small nicety of behaviour; a nice point of exactness.' *To* or *in the smallest punctilio* means 'absolutely thoroughly' (generally in an approving sense), but a *punctilio* may also be an exasperating cavil of little moment.

Punctilio can also be a general sense of fastidious propriety, the insistence that things be done exactly *comme il faut*. It is in this sense that John Updike, born on this day in 1932, uses it in his 1978 novel *The Coup*, where the narrator, in a fictional Islamic country of sub-Saharan Africa, notices some art nouveau patterns stamped on a metal door. 'These noodly motifs the French had brought,' he observes, 'along with military science, the metric system, and *punctilio*.'

Ingurgitate

To gobble greedily is to *ingurgitate*, because the Latin *gurges* means 'a whirlpool', and so *ingurgitare* means 'to pour or flood in', and so 'to gorge oneself'. It has been a favourite verb for those criticizing immoderate consumption of food or drink. The English cleric and writer of hymns, Thomas Ken – who died on this day in 1711 – was stern in his judgement of 'those sots' (or drunkards) who 'view sparkling Wines with ravish'd Eyes', and who 'Flask after Flask *ingurgitate*, till drown'd / In their own Spews they wallow on the Ground'. He would be pleased to know that no such thing occurs among modern students or vacationers.

Pannicle

While the first of March counts as the first day of meteorological spring in most of the northern hemisphere, astronomical spring – which depends on the exact tilt of the Earth and its relation to the Sun – does not begin until 19, 20, or 21 March, depending on the year, so around this day let us celebrate its arrival with the old word *pannicle*.

From the Latin for 'little cloth', *pannicle* denotes a membrane or thin layer of tissue in an animal or plant; in extended use it can also refer to the human skull, or a sheet of anything. Wallace Stevens employs it seasonally, in his poem 'The Comedian as the Letter C' (1923): 'The spring came there in clinking *pannicles* / Of half-dissolving frost, the summer came.' Not long now.

Dromena

For the Slovenian philosopher Slavoj Žižek, who was born
on this day in 1949, the pleasurable thing about a ritual
apparatus such as a Tibetan prayer wheel is that, in a way,
it does the praying for you: 'The beauty of it is that in my
psychological interior I can think about whatever I want.'
Prayer wheels, rosaries, sacred images, and other rituals are,
in his view, all examples of *dromena*: self-perpetuating phenomena that can be, as it were, left running by themselves.

The Greek word *dromena* literally means 'things done',
and in ancient Greek religion referred specifically to dramatic
re-enactments of the story of Demeter and her daughter
Persephone. When Persephone was kidnapped by Hades
and taken to the Underworld, the stricken Demeter caused
crops to die for a whole year. Hades returned Persephone,
but not before tricking her into eating some pomegranate
seeds, ensuring that she would have to return to his dark
kingdom every year. When that happens, Demeter goes into
mourning again, and that is why we have winter – which,
happily, is now over.

Evanid

The cherry-blossom season in Japan starts around this date each year, which is as fine a reason as any to celebrate the lovely word *evanid*, for whatever is fleeting or transient. It has the same Latin root as the equivalent *evanescent*, but may still be preferred for its more stylish brevity. The celebrated diarist John Evelyn wrote, for example, in his hugely influential 1664 book on forestry, *Sylva, or a Discourse of Forest-Trees*, that jasmine is a 'delicate and *evanid* flower', a phrase that somehow would be spoiled if one resorted to *evanescent* – a word that came later, and arguably needn't have done.

In 1751, the supplement to *Chambers's Cyclopaedia* observed that some authors used the word *evanid* to describe 'those flowers of plants whose petals fall off as soon as they are opened'. Others, to this day, might apply to it to those houseplants that die as soon as the owner looks in the other direction.

Acnestis

You know that bit of your upper back, right between the shoulder blades, that you can't quite scratch satisfactorily? Itches in said area might be made a smidgeon more tolerable once you know that it has a name: the *acnestis*, from the Greek for both 'unscratchable' and 'backbone'. We first find the word in the *Medicinal Dictionary* of 1745 compiled by the physician Robert James (and recommended by his friend Samuel Johnson). '*Acnestis*,' James explains, is 'that Part of the Spine of the Back, which reaches from ... the Part betwixt the Shoulder-blades, to the Loins. This Part seems to have been originally called so in Quadrupeds only, because they cannot reach it to scratch.'

James also promoted his own patent fever remedies, for which he was in some quarters accused of quackery, but then this was the eighteenth century. And so on this day, the anniversary of his death in 1776, let us at least thank him for scratching a lexical itch with *acnestis*.

Fallax

Dictionaries say that *fallax* is just an obsolete form of the word *fallacy*, both deriving from the Latin *fallax* ('false'), but the modern way *fallacy* is used – to mean some idea that, though widely held, is untrue – leaves some room for the alternative. Glossing Francis Bacon, Thomas Blount defines a *fallax* as 'a thing that's apt to deceive', and it is this sense of something actively deceptive, a trap lurking in wait for the unwary, that seems worth preserving. The poet Fulke Greville, for example, refers to 'that ever-betraying *Fallax* of undervaluing our enemies', where we would not today say exactly that it was a 'fallacy' to underestimate one's opponent.

John Gadbury, the astrologer and scientist (for in those days it was possible to be both) who died on this day in 1704, wrote, of people who allowed theory to override the evidence of their own senses: 'Who to such *Sophistry* their *Reason* bow, / Lift *Fallax* up, and set the *Truth* below.' Deliberate elevation of *fallax* remains much in evidence today.

Scrannel

In Milton's *Lycidas* (1637), Camus (a personification of the river Cam, which runs through Cambridge) takes a dim view of inexperienced shepherds who prefer to play tunes rather than making sure their livestock have enough food: 'And when they list [please], their lean and flashy songs / Grate on their *scrannel* pipes of wretched straw, / The hungry sheep look up, and are not fed.' Poor sheep. *Scrannel* is an old word for 'thin' or 'meagre', perhaps from the Norwegian for 'shrivelled'. The sense then expanded to mean 'unpleasant'; or as Dr Johnson defines it: 'Vile; worthless. Perhaps grating by the sound.'

Indeed, *scrannel* was usually applied to sounds: to people's voices, or to bad music. The English poet Anna Seward, who died on this day in 1809, complained to a correspondent about a man whose voice had a '*scrannel* tone'. Austin Dobson, meanwhile, wrote in his poem 'A Miltonic Exercise': 'In this Cash-cradled Age, / We grate our *scrannel* Musick, and we dote.' That was in 1908, but could pass in any age for a complaint about the rubbish that young people listen to these days.

26 March

Quincunx

If you plant four trees so that each is at the vertex of a square, and then plant another right in the middle, you have planted in *quincunx* formation. This word comes from the Latin for 'five-twelfths': so five trees, but twelve what? For a time, Roman currency was issued in the value of five-twelfths of an *as* or *libra* (pound), and such a coin would be marked with a pattern of five dots arranged as on the side of a die, and known as a *quincunx*.

A 1538 dictionary explains *quincunx* picturesquely thus: 'an order of setting of trees in a garden or orchard very exactly, that which way soever that a man did look, the trees stood directly one against another'. The compiler was Sir Thomas Elyot, a diplomat, scholar, and early champion of education for women, who died on this day in 1546.

Calidity

The physician Tobias Venner, who was the first man to write a whole book about the healing properties of the Bath spas, also wrote a work entitled *Via Recta ad Vitam Longam* (*The Right Way to a Long Life*), in which he counselled: 'a temperate mediocrity in *calidity*, frigidity, humidity, and siccity [dryness], as much as possibly may be; besides the lucid and clear substance of it, is for the preservation of health to be desired, because such air doth cause and conserve the health of the inhabitants'.

Calidity means 'warmth' (from the Latin *calidus*), and the ancient Roman form of central heating had heat from a basement furnace circulate through flues called *caliducts*. In English, *calid* is a nice poetic alternative to 'hot'; thus the nineteenth-century poet Sydney Dobell writes of summer personified: 'Her hot feet slippered in the *calid* seas'. Our spa-going doctor Tobias Venner, meanwhile, died on this day in 1660, at the age of eighty-two, so he might have been on to something.

Mumpish

To be *mumpish* is to be sullen and sulky: as, one hears, are many writers before their morning pint of coffee has been consumed. The word arises because a *mump* was originally a grimace or scowl, maybe from Icelandic *mump*, or 'murmur'. (The colloquial term for one of several possible infections, to *have the mumps*, came about because the characteristic swellings made the face look this way.) The splendidly descriptive *mumpish* first arises in Nathan Bailey's 1721 dictionary, crops up in the surprisingly modern-sounding insult 'you *mumpish* son of a bitch' in 1756, and has been used with pleasure by writers ever since.

Virginia Woolf, who died on this day in 1941, wielded it with particular aplomb in a 1932 letter to her sister Vanessa Bell, commiserating with her on the action of a mutual acquaintance: 'Barbara takes the cake. Never never can there have been a woman so sealed from birth to all the subtleties, sensibilities and harmonies of civilised life. To dump her *mumpish* brat on you at the last moment seems the last straw.' We've all known someone like Barbara.

Cacography

The rector Charles Butler, who died on this day in 1647, is most remembered for his 1609 book *The Feminine Monarchie, or, A Treatise Concerning Bees*, for which he became known as the father of English beekeeping. But he was also an early advocate for spelling reform. Explaining how the vowels *ou* differed in sound from word to word in English, he wrote: 'The cause of this *cacography* which causeth such difficulty is a causeless affectation of the French dialect.'

From the Greek *kakos*, 'bad', and *graphia*, 'writing', *cacography* literally means 'bad writing', either in the sense of weird spelling, as Butler meant it, or in terms of ugly handwriting. (In the latter sense it is the precise opposite of *calligraphy*, Greek for 'beautiful writing'.) But Thomas Blount suggests a third sense: 'writing of evil things'. In which case, though handwriting itself may have become rare, *cacography* is still very much abroad.

Cryptobiont

A *cryptobiont* is an organism that lives hidden from the world, as we all wish to do from time to time. From the Greek *crypto–* ('secret', hence *cryptography*, or 'secret writing') and *biont* ('kind of life'), the term *cryptobiont* is not recorded in print until 1953, perhaps because the animals it applied to had been so hard to find. It was used in a paper enticingly titled 'Revisionary Studies in the Ant Tribe Dacetini' by the Harvard zoologist and ant specialist William L. Brown, who died on this day in 1997, and whom E. O. Wilson subsequently eulogized for his 'devotion to his art'.

Cryptobionts (which can also be organisms able to live in a state of suspended animation until conditions improve) have since been found lurking in corals, crannies in rocks, and unsuspected nooks of houses where the resident *grimalkin* (see 30 December) has cleverly concealed itself.

31 March

Prevaricate

In modern usage, *prevaricate* is most often used as a synonym for 'procrastinate', to mean to delay or put off something. This is a shame, since it is an excellent word for something quite different and hardly less common: to act or speak in an evasive manner. The poet John Donne, who died on this day in 1631, warns in a theological text sternly advising his readers not to follow the unforgiving creed of the Anabaptists: 'follow not these men in their severity ... nor in their facility to disguise and *prevaricate* in things that are'.

To *prevaricate*, then, is to muddle the subject, to go off on tangents, or refuse to answer the question. So, later, Ambrose Bierce in his *Devil's Dictionary* (1906): '*Prevaricate*: To say that "she has expressive eyes", when a friend asks if you think his girl is handsome.' In modern times, a politician being interviewed may be relied upon to give a masterclass in the dubious art of *prevarication*.

APRIL

1 April

Taradiddle

This is a special day set aside for prankish untruths, but the rest of the year is hardly free of fibs, falsehoods, fabrications, and fairy tales. History, seeing that it is so badly needed, furnishes the perfect word for a person who is in the habit of telling petty lies: a *taradiddler*. In 1828 it was written of one unfortunate soul, 'His enemies ... squibbed, and paragraphed, and *taradiddled* him to death,' no doubt the fate of many victims of malevolent scribblers.

The noun *taradiddle*, for the lie itself, is attested from 1796, in *Grose's Classical Dictionary of the Vulgar Tongue*, where it is defined as 'a fib, or falsity'. Lexicographers find the etymology obscure: perhaps from *diddle* meaning 'to cheat', with the phatic exclamation *tara!* bolted on the front. In 1885 the English biologist Thomas Henry Huxley, known as 'Darwin's bulldog' for his championing of the evolutionary theory, wrote to a friend: 'Everybody told us it would be very cold, and, as usual, everybody told taradiddles.' From the 1970s *taradiddle* was also occasionally used as a synonym for mere nonsense or twaddle, but it seems more useful in the former sense, where it is close to the careful definition, by the philosopher Harry Frankfurt, of *bullshit*.

2 APRIL

Persiflage

Banter having become overused and abused, to the point where its primary use is now as a plea in self-defence for vicious and insulting speech ('It was just banter'), we need a new term for amusing badinage, or light-hearted mockery. Luckily one already exists: *persiflage*. This is an inspired borrowing from French, where the verb *persiffler* – literally, 'to whistle through [one's lips]' – has since the eighteenth century meant 'to take the piss'.

In English, *persiflage* has, over the centuries, covered the spectrum of chatter, from sneering, to urbane wit, good-humoured irony, and perhaps flirtation. In 1942 the Canadian-born travel writer Hulbert Footner – born on this day in 1879 – complained of a Maryland restaurant in which the café-style arrangement 'deprives you of the opportunity to exchange a bit of *persiflage* with the charming waitresses'. Whether the waitresses themselves were, by contrast, relieved at such deprivation is not recorded.

3 April

Ostomachy

If you have a fishbone stuck in your throat, you are engaged unwittingly or not in a form of *ostomachy*, which means 'a playing or fighting with bones' (*Glossographia*, 1656). From the Greek for 'battle' and 'bone' – in Byzantine Greece, it was a particular game played with fourteen bones – *ostomachy* is a surprisingly little-used word, given that it is one of the favourite pastimes of dogs the world over, and since it could once also describe playing or gambling with dice, which once were all made of bone. The future Henry IV – who, according to some sources, was born on this day in 1367 – had a weakness for such battles, even though the bones often beat him: he is recorded as having lost at dice in Prussia, France, and Poland. Later the inventor of logarithms, the sixteenth-century mathematician John Napier, also created a calculating device made from rods and discs of bone that was known as Napier's Bones, a contraption itself that no doubt inspired many occasions of *ostomachy*.

For the icthyological *ostomachy* previously mentioned, Judaic tradition advises you to hold the fish it came from (or the empty plate) over your head, while reciting: 'Thou art stuck in like a pin, thou art locked up as [in] a cuirass; go down, go down.' Luckily, it is a battle most people win.

Operose

When you are sighing with the overwhelming tedium of some task or book, reach for the evocative complaint term *operose*, defined by a weary Samuel Johnson as 'Laborious; full of trouble and tediousness' – as we may suspect he at times found the compilation of his own famous *Dictionary*, first published on this day in 1755.

Operose comes simply from the Latin *opus* meaning work (like the plural *opera*), and was originally applied to persons, to mean simply hard-working or industrious. Subsequently it shifted to the products of much hard work, and therefore came to mean 'boring' and 'wearisome'. In an 1855 letter, George Eliot gently admonishes her correspondent that some sentences seem '*operose* and unwieldy. Ease is the grand desideratum, next to clearness.' Both of which, of course, the great Dr Johnson had in rich abundance.

5 APRIL

Contumacy

Contumacy – from the Latin *contumax*, 'obstinate' or 'insolent' – is a stubborn-sounding word for stubbornness, or the kind of heroic resistance to authority that so many great people have exhibited, not excluding the philosopher Socrates. (In the words of the great Scottish scholar John Stuart Blackie, Socrates was sentenced to death for his *contumacy* towards the judges.)

The philosopher Thomas Hobbes, born on this day in 1588, uses it to mean something like inertia. As long as the senses are stirred with some particular stimulus, he argued, 'they are, by reason of the *contumacy* which the motion they have already gives them against the reception of all other motion, made the less fit to receive any other impression'. That is, if you are concentrating on trying to parse a knotty sentence by Thomas Hobbes, you might not notice a bird singing in the background.

Defatigable

If you are prone to tiredness – and these days, who isn't? – you may find it reassuring to know that it is all part of the cosmic plan. At least according to the theologian Joseph Glanvill, who in his *Lux Orientalis* (1662) explained: 'We were made on set purpose *defatigable*, that so all degrees of life might have their exercise.' From the Latin for 'able to be tired out', *defatigable* is, of course, the opposite of *indefatigable*, which paradoxically appears earlier in the record – but, happily, earlier than that we find, in 1533, the active verb *defatigate*, 'to exhaust', oneself or others.

'Oh what a languor runs through all my *defatigated* limbs,' exclaims one character in *Pandion and Amphigenia* (1665), by the playwright John Crowne, (baptized on this day in 1641), and one knows what he means. Historically, at least, tiredness is the primary condition, and not to be so is a peculiar and unnatural later invention.

Ingurgitate

To gobble greedily is to *ingurgitate*, because the Latin *gurges* means 'a whirlpool', and so *ingurgitare* means 'to pour or flood in', and so 'to gorge oneself'. It has been a favourite verb for those criticizing immoderate consumption of food or drink. The English cleric and writer of hymns, Thomas Ken – who died on this day in 1711 – was stern in his judgement of 'those sots' (or drunkards) who 'view sparkling Wines with ravish'd Eyes', and who 'Flask after Flask *ingurgitate*, till drown'd / In their own Spews they wallow on the Ground'. He would be pleased to know that no such thing occurs among modern students or vacationers.

Pannicle

While the first of March counts as the first day of meteorological spring in most of the northern hemisphere, astronomical spring – which depends on the exact tilt of the Earth and its relation to the Sun – does not begin until 19, 20, or 21 March, depending on the year, so around this day let us celebrate its arrival with the old word *pannicle*.

From the Latin for 'little cloth', *pannicle* denotes a membrane or thin layer of tissue in an animal or plant; in extended use it can also refer to the human skull, or a sheet of anything. Wallace Stevens employs it seasonally, in his poem 'The Comedian as the Letter C' (1923): 'The spring came there in clinking *pannicles* / Of half-dissolving frost, the summer came.' Not long now.

Dromena

or the Slovenian philosopher Slavoj Žižek, who was born on this day in 1949, the pleasurable thing about a ritual apparatus such as a Tibetan prayer wheel is that, in a way, it does the praying for you: 'The beauty of it is that in my psychological interior I can think about whatever I want.' Prayer wheels, rosaries, sacred images, and other rituals are, in his view, all examples of *dromena*: self-perpetuating phenomena that can be, as it were, left running by themselves.

The Greek word *dromena* literally means 'things done', and in ancient Greek religion referred specifically to dramatic re-enactments of the story of Demeter and her daughter Persephone. When Persephone was kidnapped by Hades and taken to the Underworld, the stricken Demeter caused crops to die for a whole year. Hades returned Persephone, but not before tricking her into eating some pomegranate seeds, ensuring that she would have to return to his dark kingdom every year. When that happens, Demeter goes into mourning again, and that is why we have winter – which, happily, is now over.

Evanid

The cherry-blossom season in Japan starts around this date each year, which is as fine a reason as any to celebrate the lovely word *evanid*, for whatever is fleeting or transient. It has the same Latin root as the equivalent *evanescent*, but may still be preferred for its more stylish brevity. The celebrated diarist John Evelyn wrote, for example, in his hugely influential 1664 book on forestry, *Sylva, or a Discourse of Forest-Trees*, that jasmine is a 'delicate and *evanid* flower', a phrase that somehow would be spoiled if one resorted to *evanescent* – a word that came later, and arguably needn't have done.

In 1751, the supplement to *Chambers's Cyclopaedia* observed that some authors used the word *evanid* to describe 'those flowers of plants whose petals fall off as soon as they are opened'. Others, to this day, might apply to it to those houseplants that die as soon as the owner looks in the other direction.

Backfriend

The word *frenemy*, denoting someone who is both a friend and an enemy, is of surprisingly long vintage, first recorded in 1953, but it does not do quite the same job as the old term *backfriend*, attested since 1472. The *OED* suggests its etymology thus: 'Perhaps originally a friend who "kept back" and did not come forward to assist, and so was no real friend', but we might prefer the more pithy explanation by Dr Johnson: 'A friend backwards; that is, an enemy in secret.'

Francis Ford Coppola was born on this day in 1939, in honour of which one might suggest a twist to Michael Corleone's line in *The Godfather Part II*: hold your friends close, but your *backfriends* closer.

8 April

Ikigai

Lorenzo de' Medici, who died on this day in 1492, had always known that the Florentine Republic was to be his plaything as it was his grandfather's and his father's before him: to rule it was his *ikigai*, or whatever gives your life meaning or motivation. A Japanese word, it originally meant 'the value of being alive', and was then adopted in this sense at the beginning of the twentieth century. Like the Danish *hygge* (roughly, 'cosiness'), *ikigai* has of late become a lifestyle trend in anglophone countries, but it is a more fundamental term. (Your *ikigai* might be to live in permanent *hygge*, or it might be to climb mountains and whatnot.)

One would hesitate to say that *ikigai* means exactly the same thing as *raison d'être* (French, 'reason to be'); on the one hand it has the idea of a vocation or calling (and so closer to *métier* in French), but it can also describe small daily pleasures such as drinking coffee in the sun. You can have only one *raison d'être* but, happily, the more *ikigai* the merrier.

9 April

Dicacity

Mockery or raillery, indulged in a good-humoured manner, can be termed *dicacity*, from the Latin *dicax* meaning 'sarcastic'. (Dr Johnson defines *dicacity* as 'pertness; sauciness', correctly for the time: those words used to be strongly negative terms for insolence or impudence, before they acquired milder, sexual overtones.) The politician and pioneering natural philosopher Francis Bacon described the Roman emperor Vespasian as 'a man exceedingly given to the humor of *dicacity* and jesting', in a pamphlet now known as *A Conference of Pleasure*, and supposed to have been given before the Court of Queen Elizabeth in 1592. Bacon died on this day in 1626, having caught a severe chill after experimenting with freezing a chicken using snow, but one suspects this towering intellect also enjoyed some *dicacity* from time to time.

10 April

Criticaster

Writers through the ages have loved to insult critics, even if they also worked as critics themselves, as did the poet and reviewer Algernon Charles Swinburne, who died on this day in 1909. Here he is in 1872, arguing that nonetheless he should certainly not be counted among 'the rancorous and reptile crew of poeticules who decompose into *criticasters*'. A *criticaster* is a small or bad critic, an impostor who does not deserve the true title; similarly, the more common *poetaster*, coined by Ben Jonson (see 21 December), and enthusiastically adopted thereafter, means a 'trashy poet'.

Handily, the suffix *–aster*, which in Latin denotes inexact likeness and so, in English, inferiority, may be applied to many other words. Extant are, for instance, *philosophaster*, *grammaticaster*, and *politicaster*, all terms – like *criticaster* – that do not lack for objects today.

11 APRIL

Granfalloon

The American novelist Kurt Vonnegut died on this day in 2007. In his novel *Cat's Cradle*, the characters practise a humane religion known as Bokononism, which is full of kindness and political satire. One of its key concepts is that of a *granfalloon*, which is a collection of people who have nothing in common besides some superficial trivialities, such as belonging to the same company or country. So the category of 'Americans' or of 'writers' is a *granfalloon*: a misleading grouping about which we cannot say anything useful because its members are all so different.

By contrast, the novel defines a *karass* as a true group of people who are like-minded and spiritually connected despite apparent differences: they might be aficionados of heavy metal, for example, or improbable lovers. Much misery arises from mistaking a *granfalloon* for a *karass*. Examples of such deceptive *granfalloons* given in *Cat's Cradle* include 'the Communist party, the Daughters of the American Revolution, the General Electric Company, the International Order of Odd Fellows – and any nation, anytime, anywhere'.

12 April

Sodality

It is at least conceivable that if there were more words in general use for love of one's fellow human beings, there might by some sociolinguistic magic be an increase in that sentiment, in hope of which we might adopt the charming word *sodality*. It comes from the Latin *sodalis*, for 'mate' or 'comrade', and denotes particularly a sense of civilized fellowship or companionship. The poet and classical scholar Thomas Stanley (himself a much-loved man), who died on this day in 1678, offers a taxonomy in his *History of Philosophy* (1656): 'Of Friendship there are *four* kinds: *Sodality*, *Affinity*, *Hospitality*, *Erotick* … The first is derived from *conversation*; the second from *nature*; the third from *cohabitation*; the fourth from *affection*.' Deriving as it does from conversation, and being particularly applied to the salon culture of the eighteenth and nineteenth centuries, then, *sodality* is a particularly literary kind of of friendship.

Airling

The lovely term *airling* was once a name for 'A young, light, thoughtless, gay person' (Johnson), and used this way by Ben Jonson in his 1611 play *Catiline*, though authorities disagree on the derivation. The grammarian John Ash, who was buried on this day in 1779, is remembered for his *A New and Complete Dictionary of the English Language* (1775), which was the first to include the words *fuck* and *cunt*: on the present matter, it says that *airling* should properly be spelled *earling* (presumably from *early*). The *OED*, however, assumes that it is straightforwardly from *air*, so meaning 'light as air'. That is presumably why the other sense of *airling* is of a creature that lives in, or travels through, the air: either a celestial fairy, or a swinging monkey. In any case, such are the insults that older generations routinely visit on the younger, sage heads might do better to say of their inheritors no worse than that they are *airlings*.

Katabasis

The grand old Duke of York, he of the ten thousand men marching up and down a hill, executed first an *anabasis* and then a *katabasis*. The first means to go up; the second means to go down, both from the Greek. And so *katabasis* came to mean various types of descent, both physical and metaphorical. Heroes who descend to the underworld, such as Orpheus or Jesus, are undergoing *katabasis*. And the term is also used for a long military retreat or flight from the enemy. In his *Anabasis*, the Greek philosopher and soldier Xenophon tells the story of the Persian Expedition, which ends in failure deep within enemy territory, necessitating a long and heroic *katabasis* by the Greek forces he now co-commands.

In modern times, the Lost Fleet series of novels by Jack Campbell, a pen name of the American writer John G. Hemry – who was born on this day in 1956 – transplants the trope of an epic *katabasis* narrative into deep space, as a group of ambushed ships struggles to fight its way home across the stars. Xenophon himself might approve.

Illaqueate

If something is ensnared, entangled, or entrapped, it is *illaqueated*. From the Latin *laqueus*, a 'noose' or 'snare', it is a word that might be recommended for its mazy emphasis. So, for instance, Satan does not merely ensnare people, he *illaqueates* them – at least, according to the lawyer and historian Edward Hall, a favourite of Henry VIII, who is thought to have died on this day in 1547. Hall wrote a posthumously published history of England entitled *The Union of the Two Noble and Illustre Families of Lancaster and York*, in which he warns: 'The devil is wont with such witchcrafts, to wrap and *illaqueate* the minds of men.'

One can also be, according to later writers, *illaqueated* by error or confusion, or alternatively by 'scholastic retiary versatility of logic'. In this splendid phrase, Coleridge doubles down on the metaphor of a snare with the fine word *retiary*, meaning 'like a net'. In our time, perhaps, fake news and conspiracy theories do not merely hoodwink their consumers, but *illaqueate* them.

16 APRIL

Petecure

The physician and naturalist Sir Hans Sloane, who was born on this day in 1660, was a collector of botanical and geological specimens, and also of manuscripts, and his collection later formed part of the core early holdings of the British Museum. But it wasn't till 1862 that one of those manuscripts was deciphered and published: a medieval cookbook entitled *Liber Cure Cocorum*, dating from about 1430. It contains the first recorded reference to 'humble pie' (or rather, as it was written at the time, pie made from *numbles*, i.e. offal), and is also the source for the rather wonderful word *petecure*, which means 'simple cooking'. 'Of *petecure* I will preach,' the unknown author announces, saying he is doing so for poor people who may not have the full array of spices necessary for more sophisticated cookery.

Petecure might remind you of its opposite, the gourmandizing *epicure*, but there is no etymological relation: the later comes from the name of the philosopher Epicurus, while *petecure* comes from the French *petit* ('small') plus *cury*, meaning 'cookery' or 'kitchen' (from the Latin *cocus*, 'cook'). There is still a street in Cambridge called Petty Cury, which in the fourteenth century was spelled Le Petycure, probably indicating 'small kitchen'. And in this age of rampant, conspicuous *gulosity* (see 29 October), perhaps the art of *petecure* deserves revival.

Gallimaufry

A *gallimaufry* was originally a kind of ragout or hash, a dish in which different kinds of food (especially meats) were mixed up together. Being such a pretty word, it soon acquired a metaphorical use for any kind of 'inconsistent or ridiculous medley', as Dr Johnson puts it, referring to Edmund Spenser's *The Shepheardes Calendar* (1579), in the Epistle to which Spenser hopes to purify the English language that he currently considers a 'a gallimaufry or hodge-podge of all other speeches'. *The Shepheardes Calendar* is also preceded by a short ditty addressed to the book itself, beginning 'Go little book ...', happily commencing a long tradition; it is inspired in part by the model of the Italian poet Baptista Mantuanus (aka Mantuan), born on this day in 1447.

In Shakespeare's *The Winter's Tale*, meanwhile, we see how *gallimaufry* can be used as a jealous insult: 'They have a dance, which the wenches say is a *gallimaufry* of gambols, because they are not in't.' For the word's derivation, the *OED* points to the French *galimafrée* before giving up the ghost: 'of unknown origin'. Happily, the French dictionary *Larousse* can explain further: it comes from the old French *galer* ('to amuse oneself') and *mafrer* ('to eat'). Satisfyingly, then, the word *gallimaufry* is itself a *gallimaufry*.

Subeth

To describe the deepest and most satisfying possible repose, one may say one slept like a dog, a baby, or the dead; a more poetic method would be to revive the word *subeth*. Rather unfairly, it has been used in English to describe sleep of an excessively or pathologically deep kind: historically, *subeth* is 'false reste' (1398), or a cousin to 'lethargy' and 'catalepsie' (1682). In the play *Any Thing for a Quiet Life* (1632), by Thomas Middleton – who was baptized on this day in 1580 – and John Webster, a barber-surgeon named Sweetball advises a young man named Ralph: 'I do begin to fear you are subject to *subeth*, unkindly sleeps, which have bred oppilations [blockages] in your brain; take heed, the *symptoma* will follow, and this may come to frenzy: begin with the first cause, which is the pain of your member.' Sweetball proposes to cut off the offending member, an operation to which Ralph does not consent.

In any case, it is unjust that *subeth* has come to represent diseased sleep, since it shares the Hebrew root of Sabbath (*šābat,* to rest or stop). Sleep being a noble pursuit, we ought to have more noble names for it.

Consopiation

Sleep, as we were saying yesterday, being one of life's great consolations, it doesn't hurt to gather pretty words for it, and one of the prettiest is *consopiation*, 'the act of laying to sleep' (Dr Johnson). This word is so obscure that it doesn't even appear in the *OED*, but let's not allow that to dissuade us; Johnson can at least cite a usage by Robert Digby, in a letter to their mutual acquaintance, the poet Alexander Pope. 'A total abstinence from intemperance is no more philosophy than a total *consopiation* of the senses is repose.' One might rather admire this conception of philosophy as necessitating some intemperance from time to time.

Digby was an unlucky fellow: the second son of a baron, he became a Tory MP but was always plagued by poor health, and died unmarried at the age of only thirty-four. Pope composed his rather moving epitaph: 'Go! fair Example of untainted youth, / Of modest wisdom, and pacific truth: / Compos'd in suff'rings, and in joy sedate, / Good without noise, without pretension great ... Of softest manners, unaffected mind, / Lover of peace, and friend of human kind.' On the anniversary of his death, let us honour Digby tonight with a calm *consopiation*.

Metoposcopy

'There's no art / To find the mind's construction in the face,' says Duncan in *Macbeth* – of which the first surviving eyewitness account of a performance was on this day in 1610. Nevertheless, there is a word for it: *metoposcopy*. It first appears in a 1569 translation of Henry Cornelius Agrippa's *On the Vanity and Uncertainty of Arts and Sciences*, wherein *metoposcopy* is defined as an art that 'can foretell all men's beginnings, proceedings, and endings ... by the only beholding of the forehead'. Sometimes the whole face, but more often just the forehead (the word is Greek for 'forehead-scope') was supposed to be transparent to persons skilled in such an art.

Later on, the English writer John Aubrey writes this of a bust of Charles I: 'There was a Seam in the middle of his Fore head (downwards) which is a very ill sign in *Metoposcopie*.' Indeed it was an ill sign for Charles I, who lost both his forehead and the rest of it. From here one can see how *metoposcopy*, fashionable in the early-modern period, was in a way a forerunner of the fashion for phrenology in the nineteenth century. Old quackeries, of course, never die out, and should you wish, you can still consult a *metoposcopist* today.

21 APRIL

Eleemosynary

Charlotte Brontë was born on this day in 1816. In her novel *Shirley* (1849), the heroine's tenant, mill-owner Gérard Moore, doubts that her new charitable fund will improve the neighbourhood. '*Eleemosynary* relief never yet tranquillized the working classes,' he declares, 'it never made them grateful; it is not in human nature that it should. I suppose, were all things ordered aright, they ought not to be in a position to need that humiliating relief; and this they feel. We should feel it were we so placed.'

This splendid word *eleemosynary* means having to do with alms (both words come from the Latin *elimosina*), or dependent on alms, or in a general sense charitable. It might be preferred over *charitable* simply for its beauty, but also because it retains the specific sense – as *charitable* and the modern use of *philanthropic* do not – of helping the poor in particular, rather than any cause or organization deemed worthy.

Bumfuzzle

If you don't know the meaning of *bumfuzzle*, chances are you are *bumfuzzled* right now; but no longer – it means to bewilder or confuse. It is first recorded on this day in 1878, when a classified ad in the *Globe* newspaper of Atchison, Kansas, read: 'Don't be *bumfuzzled* by bankrupt sales, but buy straight goods of L. Frank.' Later in the same year, the *Madison Weekly Herald* called one poor politician 'the worst *bumfuzzled* man in ten States'.

The *OED* reckons the word might be a variant of *bamboozle*, taking into account the existence also of *fuzzle* (to intoxicate or confuse) and *bumbaze* (to confound or perplex). Lest you suppose that *bumfuzzle* is merely an archaic curio, I am happy to report that in 2014, the local newspaper of Piedmont, Alabama, quoted a councillor who was surprised at waste caused by overflowing water tanks: 'It just *bumfuzzles* me that this much water is lost each year.'

Amaritude

Gideon Harvey was a Dutch-born doctor and writer, educated at Oxford and Leiden, and became the royal physician to Charles II, featuring in this role in several later portraits. It is in Harvey's 1666 work *Morbus Anglicus; or, The Anatomy of Consumptions* that we find this sorrowful account of anger: 'What *amaritude* [bitterness] or acrimony [sharpness] is deprehended [detected] in Choler.' From the Latin *amarus*, 'bitter', this word had been known in print since Caxton's day, and could be used for feelings as well as physical tastes, as Blount's *Glossographia* explains: '*Amaritude* (*amaritudo*) bitterness, solitariness, grief.'

On this day in 1661, Harvey's employer Charles II was crowned King of England, so restoring the monarchy after the execution of his father. What with the coming plague, the Great Fire of London, and plots upon his life, we may assume he found the crown came with its own fair share of *amaritude* too.

Foma

Kurt Vonnegut got the idea for his novel *Cat's Cradle* (see 11 April) while working at General Electric, which was first incorporated as the Edison General Electric Company on this day in 1889. Another word famously coined in the book is the very useful term *foma*, or 'harmless untruths'. The religion of Bokonomism featured in the book opens its sacred text, *The Books of Bokonon*, by advising the reader: 'Don't be a fool! Close this book at once! It is nothing but *foma*!', and continues: 'All of the true things that I am about to tell you are shameless lies.' But human beings need falsehoods to be cheerful, and so you should 'Live by the *foma* that make you brave and kind and healthy and happy.' Which *foma* do you live by?

Froward

A person who is, shall we say, *difficult* may be more vividly described as *froward* (pronounced FROWuhd), which literally means 'turned or going away from', deriving from the Old English *frāward*. It is thus the opposite of *toward* (at first meaning 'future', or 'approaching') which in medieval times could also mean 'friendly' and 'well-disposed'. (*Forward*, meanwhile, literally means 'the thing coming before or first' and so initially referred to the front of something, before it acquired other meanings including the metaphorical one to describe bold behaviour.)

Thus a *froward* person is one whose back is metaphorically turned on an interlocutor or the polite mores of society; a stubborn contrarian or ungovernable mischief-maker. Angry cocks, judges, bad artists, and especially children have been labelled *froward* through the ages. The term is handled well by the English statesman and essayist William Temple, born on this day in 1628, in this splendid summing-up of why he defends the arts of poetry and music, though others consider them little more than paltry entertainments. 'When all is done,' Temple writes, 'Human Life is, at the greatest and the best, but like a *froward* Child, that must be play'd with and humour'd a little to keep it quiet till it falls asleep, and then the Care is over.'

Mellifluous

From the Latin *mel*, 'honey', and *fluere*, 'to flow', what is *mellifluous* is literally running with honey, or deliciously sweet. It is still occasionally used in this way, of cakes or German beer, but is more likely to appear in its metaphorical sense, usually applied to the sound of language or music, or to one who makes such sound – as, for instance, William Shakespeare, who was baptized on this day in 1564, was called '*Mellifluous* Shake-speare, whose inchanting Quill / Commanded Mirth or Passion' by his contemporary, the playwright Thomas Heywood.

In Shakespeare's *Twelfth Night*, after the clown Feste has sung a love ditty, Sir Andrew comments, approvingly: 'A *mellifluous* voice, as I am true knight.' Toby calls it a 'contagious breath', to which Andrew assents – 'Very sweet and contagious, i'faith' – before Toby succeeds in reducing their admiration to absurd bathos: 'To hear by the nose, it is dulcet in contagion.'

Subaltern

The Italian philosopher Antonio Gramsci, who died on this day in 1937, introduced the term *subaltern* into political theory to refer to oppressed and marginalized groups within a particular society. The word comes from the Latin term for 'of inferior rank', *subalternus*, and was used this way from the sixteenth century to describe subordinate jurisdictions, professions, or groups of people, as well as junior military officers. In Horace Walpole's 1764 novel *The Castle of Otranto*, the preface that introduces the supposedly found manuscript refers to the servants of the story with this term: 'Some persons may, perhaps, think the characters of the domestics too little serious for the general cast of the story; but, besides their opposition to the principal personages, the art of the author is very observable in his conduct of the *subalterns*.'

Much later, however, one of Gramsci's successors was to worry that the word had become too widely applied in politics. Many people wanted to claim the badge of *subalternity*, said the Indian scholar Gayatri Chakravorty Spivak. But, she continued, it 'is not just a classy word for "oppressed" … In post-colonial terms, everything that has limited or no access to the cultural imperialism is *subaltern* – a space of difference.'

Saltimbanco

A *saltimbanco* (or sometimes *saltinbanco*) is a quack or mounte-bank, 'an itinerant charlatan who sold supposed medicines and remedies, frequently using various entertainments to attract a crowd of potential customers' (*OED*). The word appears first in 1646, in Thomas Browne's rogues' gallery of mischievous agents of misinformation: '*Saltimbancoes*, Quacksalvers, and Charlatans'. The poet and translator Charles Cotton, who was born on this day in 1630, employs it with divine lèse-majesté in his *Burlesque Upon Burlesque: or, The Scoffer Scoft* (1675), in which a god himself is so described: '*Apollo, Jack of all Trades* is: / An *Archer, Fidler, Poetaster* [see 21 December] / A kind of *Salt'in-banco* too.'

The original Spanish word *saltinbanco* is derived from the Italian *saltare in banco*, which literally means 'to leap onto a bench', as the travelling quack would do in the street to attract an audience. (Happily, *mountebank* means exactly the same thing, formed from the Italian *monta in banco*.) Today's *saltimbancos*, of course, have no need of such physical exertion.

Enthymeme

An incomplete argument, where some premise is missing or actively suppressed, is called an *enthymeme*, a term mainly used in academic philosophy, as well as by people making fun of academic philosophy. One of those was the Scottish satirist John Arbuthnot, not as famous now as his friends Swift and Pope, who was baptized on this day in 1667. In his *Lewis Baboon Turned Honest, Being the Fourth Part of Law is a Bottomless-Pit* (1712), Arbuthnot has the character of Don Diego declaim: 'Since those worthy Persons, who are as much concern'd for your Safety as I am, have employ'd me as their Orator, I desire to know whether you will have it by way of Syllogism, *Enthymeme*, Dilemma or Sorites.' (A sorites is a sequence of logical syllogisms in which the conclusion of one forms a premise for the next.) John Bull – for it is he, the doughty figure of an Englishman invented by Arbuthnot himself – replies, phlegmatically: 'Let's have a Sorites by all means, tho' they are all new to me.'

In our day, some writers have proposed reviving the term *enthymeme* to analyse the way in which political soundbites – such as 'death panel' – themselves contain, or smuggle in, unstated arguments. Alternatively we might call them *unspeak*, but as the author of a book of that title, the present writer might be expected to say that.

Edgelord

On this day in 1993, the public world-wide web became possible. It had been invented by the British scientist Tim Berners-Lee while working at CERN, the European nuclear-research facility, which now released the technology globally on a royalty-free basis. This is as good an anniversary as any, then, on which to celebrate, or perhaps lament, the multifarious human types who came into existence thanks to modern digital communications. Among the most anarchic of such personalities is that of the *edgelord*, a term in popular use since 2015.

An *edgelord* is someone (usually a man) who posts on internet forums and social media with the express intent of being as 'edgy' as possible, expressing the most nihilistic or outrageous opinions he can think of. The implication of nobility in *edgelord* is thus meant ironically, to indicate that such posters only believe they are superior to others. For the potency of its paradoxically belittling contempt, it seems an excellent word to apply more widely, in case one feels that the ranks of public intellectuals, commentators, and other bloviators are themselves increasingly populated by *edgelords*.

MAY

1 May

Juvescence

Welcome to the month of May, which according to T. S. Eliot's poem 'Gerontion' (1920) is 'depraved'. The poem contains one of only two examples ever recorded of the word *juvescence*. (The other was by Stephen Spender, twenty-eight years later.) In 'Gerontion' we read: 'In the juvescence of the year / Came Christ the tiger / In depraved May, dogwood and chestnut, flowering judas ...' The more common version of the word is *juvenescence*, meaning simply 'youth'. In 1989, Anthony Burgess was reviewing the second edition of the *OED*, and peevishly picked on this entry. Eliot 'was wrong', Burgess wrote. 'It should be "juvenescence". His authority prevails, and we can dishonour Latin etymology as we wish. The *OED* bestows the right.'

One might reply that Eliot's *juvescence* fits the metre where *juvenescence* would not, and it also seems a more natural opposite to *senescence* (age). Moreover, Eliot might have intended a more precise relation to the Latin root: *juvenis* was a man or woman specifically of post-adolescent age rather than just 'young', which after all makes more sense when applied to the fifth month of the year.

Cocqcigrues

The Reverend E. Cobham Brewer was the mastermind of *Brewer's Dictionary of Phrase and Fable*, in the 1895 revised edition of which we find this curious entry: '*Cocqcigrues. At the coming of the Cocqcigrues.* That good time coming, when every mystery shall be cleared up.' For authority he cites Charles Kingsley's *The Water Babies*, where a fairy remarks that there are seven things 'I am forbidden to tell till the coming of the Cocqcigrues'. A *Cocqcigrue* (pronounced cockSEEgruh) is a purely imaginary, absurd animal, and is first encountered in Rabelais, where 'the coming of the *Cocqcigrues* ('à la venue des *cocquecigrues*') means simply . . . never. Just as you would never see a bird that was a mashup of a cock, a crane, and a stork (*coque, grue, cigogne*). So it seems that the Revd Brewer, born on this day in 1810, might have misinterpreted Kingsley's line; but no matter, let us wish him a happy birth anniversary nonetheless.

Fantysheeny

Chiefly found in the old dialect of Devon, the word *fantysheeny* means 'fancy' or 'ostentatious', as first recorded in *Letters and Poems in the Devonshire Dialect* (1847), by Nathan Hogg, where a lustful narrator remarks: 'Exeter maidens luke well anuff wen thay be dress'd, / Way thare vine *vantysheeny* goold things in thare brest.' Pleasingly, the word is a direct borrowing of the Italian *fantoccini*, meaning 'little puppets'.

'Nathan Hogg' was actually the pseudonym of Henry Baird, an Exeter law clerk, journalist, and bookseller, who died on this day in 1881. Such was the popularity of his *Letters* that Baird received a visit from a passionate philologist who commissioned him to translate the Song of Solomon into the Devonshire tongue – none other than Prince Louis Lucien Bonaparte, a nephew of Napoleon. Now that's pretty *fantysheeny*.

Rhinocerize

The Israeli novelist Amos Oz, born on this day in 1939, is credited with introducing into Hebrew the concept of *rhinocerization* with the verb *lehitkarnef* and its adjective *meitkarnef*. The choice of animal is inspired by Eugène Ionesco's 1959 play *Rhinoceros*, in which the inhabitants of a small French town gradually turn into rhinoceroses, in an allegory of conformity under Nazi occupation. 'In one of my articles,' Oz remembered, 'I invented the verb "to rhinocerize" or the noun "rhinocerized" to describe a man who becomes conformist, who changes his or her opinions in order to adjust to a certain general mood or certain general trend.'

In Hebrew the word's meaning has now mutated so that it can denote having a thick skin, being brutish, or behaving boorishly on the dancefloor. But if we still need a word for what Oz described as the 'opportunistic tendency of many people to adjust to a totalitarian system', we could do worse than to promote *rhinocerize* in English.

Desiderium

If you once had a thing – perhaps a favourite T-shirt or *inamoratus* – that is now lost to you, and you think of it with longing, you are experiencing a *desiderium*. It comes from the Latin *desiderare*, to miss or long for – which, evocatively, the *OED* suggests might be etymologically connected with *sider*, 'star'. (If you are afflicted by loss, have your stars abandoned you?)

Jonathan Swift knew the pangs of it well, having moved from London to Dublin, and thereafter, as he wrote to Pope apologetically, having not replied to him for a while: 'When I leave a country without probability of returning, I think as seldom as I can of what I loved or esteemed in it, to avoid the *desiderium* which of all things makes life most uneasy.' Swift made his last will on this day in 1740, which included his own epitaph: 'Here lies the body of Jonathan Swift, Doctor of Sacred Theology, Dean of this Cathedral, where savage indignation can no longer tear at his heart. Pass on, traveller, and, if you can, emulate his tireless efforts in defence of liberty.'

Stockjobber

On this day in 2008, the *Wall Street Journal* carried an interview about trouble in the mortgage-banking business with US Treasury Secretary Hank Paulson, who said: 'I do believe that the worst is likely to be behind us.' Four months later, Lehman Brothers filed for bankruptcy, precipitating the global financial crash. Perhaps it is time to readjust the amount of rhetorical respect we pay to financial traders by resurrecting the plain term *stockjobber*. Dr Johnson defines it, magisterially, as: 'A low wretch who gets money by buying and selling shares in the funds.'

Thomas Shadwell's 1692 play *The Volunteers, Or, The Stock-Jobbers: A Comedy*, features two such low wretches, who attempt to persuade their clients to buy shares in such dubious projects as a patent for walking underwater, or a remedy that can kill all the fleas in every family in England. 'It's no matter in the end whether it turns to use or not,' one of them explains; 'the main end verily is to turn the penny in the way of stock jobbing, that's all.'

Mollitious

This is a decadent-sounding word for a decadent thing. Sensuousness or luxury is what deserves the name of *mollitious* (from the Latin for 'softness'), used in judgements both disapproving and rather excited. The poet Robert Browning, born on this day in 1812, used it in his long poem *Sordello*: '*mollitious* alcoves gilt / Superb as Byzant-domes the devils built.' That is far from being among the poem's most obscure lines. The then poet laureate, Lord Tennyson, remarked of Browning's effort: 'There were only two lines in it that I understood, and they were both lies; they were the opening and closing lines, "Who will may hear Sordello's story told", and "Who would has heard Sordello's story told".' Rather too bitchy, one might object: knotted and puzzling it might be, but *Sordello* is also *mollitious*, if sometimes to a fault.

8 MAY

Abactor

The ruffian known as an *abactor*, from the Latin for 'to drive away', was a robber of livestock. Edward Gibbon, who was born on this day in 1737, explains that in Roman times, an *abactor* would attract the death penalty for stealing 'one horse, or two mares or oxen, or five hogs, or ten goats'. Thomas Blount's 1670 law dictionary, the *Nomo-Lexicon*, emphasizes that *abactors* were 'stealers of Cattle or Beasts, by Herds or great numbers; and were distinguished from *Fures* [common thieves]'.

In nineteenth-century America, the term came to be applied specifically to cattle thieves who operated on a large scale. In his *Devil's Dictionary*, Ambrose Bierce defines it thus: 'One who steals a whole herd of cattle, as distinguished from the inferior actor who steals one animal at a time.' In similar spirit, the term *abactor* could today be applied to the man who steals millions and gets away with it, rather than the unfortunate who steals hundreds and goes to prison.

Tachygraphy

Dr Johnson defines *tachygraphy* as 'The art or practice of quick writing', in which he himself was of course an expert, as must anyone be who is a freelance man of letters. ('No one but a blockhead,' the great man once said, 'ever wrote except for money.') Formed straightforwardly from the Greek for 'swift writing', *tachygraphy* has also been used to mean any system for getting things down more quickly, such as shorthand, or the Latin of the Middle Ages, which was full of abbreviations, *etc.* One of the earliest manuals of shorthand was Thomas Shelton's *Tachygraphy* (1639), a system that was adopted by such luminaries as Thomas Jefferson and Samuel Pepys. On this day in 1667, Pepys records a friend asking him to recommend a new assistant: 'He insists upon an unmarried man, that can write well, and hath French enough to transcribe it, only from a copy, and may write shorthand.'

Shorthand might be a vanishing skill in the digital age, but anyone today hurrying to complete an email or business report, still less a book, may still encourage themselves by noting that they are *tachygraphers*.

Obnunciation

On this day in 1940, Neville Chamberlain resigned as prime minister following the Allied debacle in Norway, and Winston Churchill was appointed by the King in his stead: hence, one might say, there was an *obnunciation* of the old government. If unfavourable auguries or evil events were on the horizon, the Romans would dissolve their assemblies. This act of dissolution, or the announcement of bad news itself, was *obnunciation*, from the Latin for 'announcement before' or 'announcement in view of'.

So, as Thomas Blount explains in his *Glossographia*, *obnunciation* came to mean 'forbidding a thing upon foreknowledge, conjecture or likelihood of its ill success'. In modern times, you might think, more acts of *obnunciation* might have averted quite a few disasters.

11 MAY

Bibliotaph

The British writer Isaac D'Israeli, born on this day in 1766, is credited – among many other things, including fathering the future prime minister Benjamin Disraeli – with coining the word *bibliotaph*, which means a person who entombs books by keeping them under lock and key. (Greek *biblios*, 'book', plus *taphos*, 'tomb'.) In 1888, William Blades published a book called *The Enemies of Books*, in which he described one sorry example: 'Sir Thomas Phillipps, of Middle Hill, was a remarkable instance of a *bibliotaph*. He bought bibliographical treasures simply to bury them. His mansion was crammed with books; he purchased whole libraries, and never even saw what he had bought.' That is certainly to be regretted, though Blades's book is enjoyably splenetic in other ways, seeing as it does the enemies of books everywhere he looks. One of the most redoubtable such foes, for example, was 'Library invaded for the purpose of dusting'. For nineteenth-century literary gentlemen, *bibliotaphs* or no, the struggle was definitely real.

12 MAY

Hunks

This is one of those words on which Dr Johnson demonstrates command of disapproving synonyms: 'A covetous sordid wretch; a miser; a curmudgeon.' So indeed meant *hunks* in English from 1602. In his play *The Spanish Fryar*, John Dryden – who died on this day in 1700 – has a character describe a woman's husband as 'a jealous, covetous, old *Huncks*'. The singular *hunk*, meaning 'large piece', is not recorded until the nineteenth century, and the sense of 'ruggedly attractive man' only arrives in the middle of the twentieth, when it supplants that of 'large person'. So why is a *hunks* a miser, in particular? The *OED* suggests: 'It has the appearance of a quasi-proper name or nickname, like Old Grumbles, Bags, Boots, and the like.' And perhaps the original source of the proper name in question was not a human at all. As of 1590, there was a bear named Tom Hunks at the Bankside bear-baiting pits, not far from Shakespeare's Globe. Perhaps *hunks* in spoken English already meant miserly, for reasons now lost, and Tom was so named for his distinctly ungenerous character; or perhaps the bear himself was so spectacularly mean that he passed eponymously into the language.

13 MAY

Yare

On this day in 1607, three English ships landed at Virginia and established Jamestown. The man who became de facto governor of the colony was John Smith, a soldier and writer, among whose publications was an influential manual for young sailors, *An Accidence, or the Path-Way to Experience, Necessary for All Young Seamen* (1626). In the chapter 'How to Manage a Fight at Sea', he advises: 'We have the wind of him, and he tacks about, tack you about also and keep your loufe [keep near the wind], be *yare* at the helm ...'

If a person is ready and eager to do something, they are *yare* (pronounced YAIR), from the Old Norse *gǫrr* meaning 'prompt' or 'skilful'. In Shakespeare's *Measure for Measure*, the bartender and pimp Pompey is hired as an executioner's assistant, and says: 'If you have occasion to use me for your own turn, you shall find me *yare*.' Since this has a sense of 'quick' and 'eager to please', *yare* can also mean 'brisk' and 'efficient in action', which is the way John Smith encouraged his readers to be in a sea-battle, and also the way Shakespeare uses it in *Antony and Cleopatra*: 'I have savage cause,' Antony declares, 'And to proclaim it civilly were like / A haltered neck [a man in a noose] which does the hangman thank / For being *yare* about him.'

Logodaedalus

On this day in 1608, the English wit and travel writer Thomas Coryat embarked on the five-month tour of Europe that was to be described in his hugely popular 1611 account, *Coryat's Crudities Hastily Gobbled Up in Five Months Travels in France, Italy, &c.* When in London he was a drinking buddy, at the Mermaid Tavern on Cheapside, of luminaries now better remembered, including John Donne, Francis Beaumont, and Ben Jonson, the last of whom heaped praise on his friend in a generous preface to *Crudities*. Coryat, Jonson wrote, was 'a great and bold Carpenter of words, or (to express him in one like his own) a *Logodædale*'. The Greek *daidalos* means 'cunning', so a *logodaedalus* is a cunning wordsmith: Jonson evidently coined the word in humorous imitation of his friend's exuberant style.

Later, the variant *logodaedalist* was briefly adopted to mean one who indulged in unnecessary new coinages: 'an Inventer or Forger of new Words, and strange Terms', as Nathan Bailey put it rather disapprovingly in his 1721 *Dictionary*. But – in Thomas Coryat's memory – it would be more pleasant to reserve *logodaedalus* as a term signalling sincere praise for uncommon artistry in writing.

Axinomancy

One cannot resist such a word as defined in Blount's *Glossographia*: 'divination or witchcraft done by Hatchets'. Obscure as such a practice might sound today, it was 'in good repute among the Ancients; and was performed by laying an Agate-stone on a red-hot Hatchet'. That, at least, is according to the English writer Ephraim Chambers – who died on this day in 1740 – in his magnificent *Cyclopaedia, or an Universal Dictionary of Arts and Sciences* (1728). Straightforwardly from the Greek for 'axe' and 'divination', *axinomancy* has also taken the recorded forms of interpreting the quivering of an axe flung into a tree or table, or observing the changing colours as it glows in a fire.

According to an 1855 compendium of the occult, meanwhile, *axinomancy* 'was performed by balancing an axe on an upright stake, and the names of suspected persons being pronounced, it was supposed to point out the guilty by its motion'. We may be thankful that modern justice is usually more reliable.

Homiletics

A homily – from the Greek *homilos*, 'a crowd' – is a religious lecture, particularly one that is aimed at improving the spiritual condition of the congregation rather than analysing some particular idea, or one that expounds on a single passage of sacred text. So *homiletics* became the name for the art of preaching, an art founded, according to one later scholar, by the writings of the Flemish theologian Andreas Hyperius, who was born on this day in 1511.

Of course, *homily* soon acquired the secondary sense of any boringly moralistic speech: a meaning already present in Shakespeare's *As You Like It*: 'What tedious homily of love,' Rosalind complains after the recitation of a bad poem. Similarly, not everyone admired the art of *homiletics*, which Ambrose Bierce defines mischievously as 'the science of adapting sermons to the spiritual needs, capacities and conditions of the congregation'. So, too, we might adopt *homiletics* to describe any number of modern discourses that seem primarily to expatiate on the speaker's own virtue.

Scrithe

The ancient word *scrithe* means to come or go, to glide, or simply to wander. It is etymologically related to the old Icelandic *skritha*, which means 'a landslip', and so also 'to creep or glide'. Thus a fifteenth-century writer might say that a feeling *scrithes* upon one, or that the unwary might *scrithe* into sinfulness. Both these examples are from the work of Richard Misyn, who was ordained deacon on this day in 1421, before becoming a hermit and translating the works of the fourteenth-century mystic monk Richard Rolle.

Alarmingly, *scrithing* in circles is something that the monsters Grendel and his mother are described as doing in *Beowulf* (in rough translation: 'men do not know where the hellish ones wander around'). On the other hand, in Old English it was often time itself that was said to be *scrithing*, which seems a gentler and less anxious picture than our modern idea of time ticking away or running out.

18 MAY

Brontology

Dr Johnson gives a poetically laconic definition of this word: '*Brontology*: A dissertation upon thunder.' Indeed, so it is: 'that part of Meteorology which treats of thunder' (*OED*), because the Greek *brontē* means thunder. (The name of the dinosaur *brontosaurus* thus means 'thunderous lizard'.) The word sounds marvellously old-fashioned, yet if by 'a dissertation upon thunder' we mean a scientific investigation into thunderstorms in general, they continue apace – the phenomenon of lightning itself is not yet fully understood. The radio-frequency discharges of lightning, known as *sferics* (short for 'atmospherics') are among the sound effects used on the first track of Pink Floyd's 1993 album *The Division Bell*. And on this day in 2015, the atmospheric scientists Steve Ackerman and Jonathan Martin wrote: 'What is brontology? Brontology is the scientific study of thunder.' Happily, then, unlike brontosauri, *brontologists* still walk among us.

Factitious

What is *factitious*, strangely, is not a *fact*. Both words derive ultimately from the Latin *facere*, to make or do, but while a fact (Latin *factum*) is something done, a *factitious* thing (Latin *facticius*) is something 'of the made sort', something manufactured or artificial – and so, in English, often deceptive, false, or inauthentic. The novelist Rebecca West, for example, remarked of St Augustine: 'He objects to stage plays, because they arouse in the audience *factitious* emotion of a hysterical and unprofitable sort.' Earlier, Nathaniel Hawthorne – who died on this day in 1864 – had complained in his travel diary of a lacklustre party in Florence: 'The Feast of St John ... is but a meagre semblance of festivity, kept alive *factitiously*, and dying a lingering death of centuries.'

Meanwhile, writers through the years have objected to factitious value, factitious tracts, and factitious political debates, the last of which show no sign of vanishing from view. Perhaps, just as *truthiness* denotes the quality of seeming but not really being true, we might employ *factitiousness* for the quality of seeming to have, but not really having, something to do with the facts.

20 MAY

Quodlibetarian

The word might not be familiar, but the world is surely more full than at any previous point in its history of *quodlibetarians*, people who express half-formed opinions on any subject under the sun. The Latin *quodlibet* means 'whatever you please', and the academic *quodlibetum* was once an exercise in which the master talked about any topic suggested by the audience. So a *quodlibetarian* is one willing to talk, as though knowledgeably, about anything at all.

The English satirist Max Beerbohm, who died on this day in 1956, used the word in fond ribbing of the philosopher C. E. M. Joad. In his biography *Lytton Strachey* (1943), Beerbohm writes: 'Not long ago I heard that agile and mellifluous *quodlibetarian*, Dr Joad, saying in answer to a questioner who wanted to write good letters, that anybody could write good letters.' Beerbohm disagreed. 'A true gift for writing ... is not widely disposed. Nor is a true gift for painting, or for playing the violin; and of that we are somehow aware. We do not say to a violinist "Just think out clearly what you want to express and then go straight ahead. Never mind how you handle your bow."' Now there was a man who could write on whatever he pleased: a true *quodlibetarian* in the best sense.

Witling

Dr Johnson defines *witling* as 'A pretender to wit; a man of petty smartness'. It is formed from *wit* plus the suffix *–ling*, which in Old Norse has a diminutive force, continued in English in words such as *gosling*, *duckling*, or *princeling*, as well as less successful formations such as *philosophling*, which may be found in the philologist James Gilchrist's 1815 book *The Labyrinth Demolished; or, The Pioneer of Rational Philology*.

Witling, though, seems profitable to this day. In his *Essay on Criticism*, Johnson's contemporary Alexander Pope – born on this day in 1688 – wrote of 'Those half-learn'd *Witlings* num'rous in our Isle, / As half-form'd Insects on the banks of Nile.' They have not grown less numerous since.

22 May

Deipnosophist

Everyone today considers themselves experts on foodie (or foodist) matters, but how many really deserve the name of *deipnosophist*? The word is formed from the Greek *deipnon* ('main meal', 'dinner') and *sophistes* ('master craftsman' or 'wise man'). Put them together and you have 'one learned in the mysteries of the kitchen' (*OED*), such as Elizabeth David, who died on this day in 1992.

The word was popularized by the Greek writer Athanaeus in the third century CE, by which time it meant not merely an excellent cook but a philosopher-eater. His book *The Deipnosophists* (which later came in English with the explanatory subtitle 'Banquet of the Learned') is a description of several banquets during which the erudite guests discuss philosophy, music, wine, sex, and the arts while scoffing as much as they can from endless platters of 'Chickens, ducks and roasted geese, goats, hares, pigeons, turtles and partridges', and so forth. Gluttony, perhaps, is vindicated by wit.

Heterophemize

Modern politicians are fond of not-quite-apologizing for unsuccessful remarks by claiming that they *misspoke*; a more rhetorically impressive defence, perhaps, would be to claim that one *heterophemized*. From the Greek for 'other speech', the original version of the word was coined by the American literary critic Richard Grant White in 1875, when writing of the unfortunate syndrome by which 'The assertion made is most often not merely something that the speaker or writer does not mean to say, but its very reverse, or at least something notably at variance with his purpose. For this reason I have called it *heterophemy*, which means merely the speaking otherwise.'

As a verb, White's simultaneous coinage *heterophemize* did not enjoy much subsequent popularity, but it usefully names something we all do from time to time, whether we use the wrong word for a common object, or accidentally insult someone. Perhaps the only person immune to *heterophemy*, indeed, is the ideal figure of the gentleman, under the old definition of 'a man who never gives offence unintentionally'.

24 MAY

Omphalos

In the temple of Apollo at Delphi sat a round conical stone that, for the Greeks, marked the centre of the Earth. It was known as the *omphalos*, which also meant 'navel'. That term was first used in English, it appears, by Thomas De Quincey in *Suspiria de Profundis* (1845), where he remarks that, before 'the figure of the planet became known', it was once claimed that Delphi was the centre of the Earth, and at another time that Jerusalem was; and for Christian people, Jerusalem remained 'the *omphalos* of mortality'. The term was adopted, too, for the creationist theory that God had deliberately made the world to look very old, even though it wasn't, by the nineteenth-century zoologist Philip Henry Gosse in his 1857 book *Omphalos: An Attempt to Untie the Geological Knot*. It met with derision, but Gosse was still defending himself in a magazine on this day in 1872, writing: 'Many have sneered at it (an easy process!) but I have not yet met with a single adversary who accepting my postulates have convicted me of non-sequitur.'

The *omphalos* theory of divine creation rather fell by the wayside, but since then, *omphalos* has still been available to indicate the centre or hub of some idea or activity, as Panama is today the *omphalos* of tax evasion.

Cynosure

The North Star or Pole Star (of the northern hemisphere) received its modern scientific name *Polaris* thanks to the Dutch scientist Gemma Frisius, who died on this day in 1555. Because of its apparent fixity ('I am constant as the northern star,' says Shakespeare's Julius Caesar), it has through the ages been an important aid to maritime navigation. Polaris is to be found in the constellation Ursa Minor, anciently named *Cynosure* (Greek for 'a dog's tail') – and so the word *cynosure* itself, in English, came to denote a guiding light, or a brilliant centre of attention.

So a pleasantly infatuated Thomas Carlyle wrote of Marie Antoinette: 'The fair young Queen, in her halls of state, walks like a goddess of Beauty, the *cynosure* of all eyes.' Meanwhile, a seventeenth-century cleric argued: 'For the guidance of our either caution, or liberty ... the only *Cynosure* is our Charity.' When the affairs of humans lack direction, a cynosure is sorely needed.

Elingued

If you are made speechless by something you may say you are *elingued*: literally, deprived of a tongue. The earlier verb form *elinguate* was said to be a practice of the devil, and the later *elinguation* was used only to refer to the literal, maiming act, usually as punishment.

But those of us fortunate enough not to be subject to *elinguation* might still often feel *elingued*. The word is first attested as used by the poet and essayist Owen Felltham in 1623, when he wrote: 'If it be by speech a man is to act his part, fear puts an ague [shake] in his tongue, and often leaves him ... quite *elingued*.' This is from his book *Resolves: Divine, Morall, Politicall*, entered into the Stationers' Register on this day in 1623, and unfortunately remains as true as ever it was.

27 MAY

Jactance

You probably know someone who indulges in *jactance*, which is a pleasingly precise term for boasting or 'vainglorious speaking', the sort of thing that often goes together with other vices, as an early sixteenth-century author put it: 'arrogance, *jactance*, & hypocrisy'. Thereafter *jactance* was used generally as any kind of boastfulness. 'Let there be no *jactance* in an epitaph,' warned the travel writer and priest Henry Digby Best, who died on this day in 1836.

It comes from the Latin for 'to throw about' (*jacere*), and if you prefer you can also use the English word *jactation*. ('There is no surer sign of vulgarity than *jactation* of gentility,' warned the *London Magazine* in 1825.) But there is something about the sound of *jactance*, reminiscent of an unpleasant, diseased oozing, that seems peculiarly appropriate to the phenomenon it describes.

Smellfeast

Early English had a pleasing habit of smashing words together to make vivid compounds, such as *seeksorrow* (Dr Johnson: 'One who contrives to give himself vexation'), and the splendid *smellfeast*: 'A parasite; one who haunts good tables.' One who is a *smellfeast* might also be a *lickplate*, who waits till the invited guests have had their fill before tonguing the leftovers. As well as the kind of human being who is a 'greedy sponger' (*OED*), creatures that have been called *smellfeasts* include the housefly, birds, and certain denominations of friar.

Noah Webster, the lexicographer who died on this day in 1843, defined *smellfeast* properly as 'One that is apt to find and frequent good tables; an epicure; a parasite' in his 1828 *American Dictionary of the English Language*. The posthumous 'unabridged' 1864 edition, however, with revisions and additions by other editors, added this rather surreal definition: 'A feast at which the guests are supposed to feed upon the odors only of the viands.' One might be forgiven for doubting that such a feast ever took place, yet that sense is still given for *smellfeast* in the modern *Merriam-Webster* dictionary. *Caveat lector.*

Phillumeny

There is a word for even the most specialized of hobbies, and *phillumeny* is just what you need to describe the collecting of matchboxes or matchbook covers. The British Matchbook Label and Bookmatch Society maintains a *phillumeny* website, and phillumenists the world over have as their patron saint the English pharmacist John Walker, born on this day in 1781. Based in Stockton-on-Tees, he invented the friction match – or what he called 'friction lights' – in 1826. Collectors of match packaging became known as *labellists*, until in 1943 a contributor to the enthusiasts' magazine *Floyd's Label Review*, one M. S. Evans, wrote to suggest a less dull name. By mixing Latin and Greek, he pointed out, he and his fellows could call themselves *phillumenists* – 'lovers of light'.

The term, as well as *phillumeny* for the activity itself, quickly caught on, and *Floyd's Label Review* renamed itself *The Phillumenist*. 'Little did John Walker foresee,' wrote a contributor to the *Listener* in 1967, 'that his invention would become a great blessing to mankind, or that it would give rise to a popular hobby – *phillumeny*.' There are not many great inventors who have also given rise to such a beautiful new word.

Hippotherapy

Dictionaries do not record whether it helps to talk to a sad hippopotamus, for *hippotherapy* is rather the practice of helping people by putting them on horses. (*Hippos* is the Greek for 'horse', and *hippopotamus* literally means 'river-horse'; *hippotherapy* is defined broadly by experts as 'the medical use of the horse'.) The word first appeared in print on this day in 1978, referring to an early example of the practice at the children's clinic of the University of Vienna. Since then, hippotherapy has been shown to improve the posture, muscle strength, and gait of people with physical difficulties, as movement is gently transferred from horse to rider, as well as to bring psychosocial benefits to the lucky equestrians.

Cognoscible

The French essayist and founding member of the Académie Française, Jean-Louis Guez de Balzac (no relation to the later novelist Honoré de Balzac) was born on this day in 1597. In his political treatise *The Prince* (1631), he observes that, as a result of corrupt and tyrannical European rulers, 'There remains nothing entire, nor *cognoscible* in Germany, but the Sea and the Mountains.' *Cognoscible* – in French, and in English once de Balzac's book was translated in 1648 – signifies something that can be known, as some scholars insisted that God was, and other scholars as fervently denied that He could be.

Later, in 1825, the philosopher Jeremy Bentham wrote that, in a just society, everyone would know exactly what the law was: 'A determinate system of *cognoscible* laws, capable of being known, is necessary. Unhappily, such a system does not yet exist.' Laws having sprouted ever faster since, such a cognoscible system seems even further off.

JUNE

1 JUNE

Alazony

The singer Alanis Morissette was born on this day in 1974; her most famous song, 'Ironic', subsequently inspired never-ending torrents of mansplaining that no, actually, rain on your wedding day isn't ironic. Arguably it is, according to the long-attested concept of situational irony. Such carpers, indeed, often themselves suffer from *alazony*, which is an excellent term for an inability to recognize irony when they see it. It derives from the ancient Greek *alazoneia* for 'boastfulness' or 'imposture', and in English originally meant generally pride or arrogance (*OED*), before it was adopted in mid-twentieth-century literary criticism for the specific fault of irony-blindness. It surely could be diagnosed more often now, when subtle jokes lead inevitably to outrage.

2 JUNE

Nimiety

On this day in 1834, Samuel Taylor Coleridge is recorded as having remarked: 'There is a *nimiety* – a too-muchness – in all Germans. It is the national fault.' (To be fair, he was talking specifically, and with amusing rudeness, about the poetry of Schiller: 'Schiller's blank verse is bad. He moves in it as a fly in a glue bottle.') But how pleasant that there exists a word for too-muchness, or 'excess, redundancy, superfluity' (*OED*).

From the Latin *nimius* ('excessive'), via the English *nimious* (ditto), *nimiety* or 'too-muchness' is the lesser-known opposite of *satiety*, meaning 'sufficiency', particularly in terms of having had enough to eat. But regrettable overindulgence at dinner is hardly the only context in which the word may earn its keep. When it's just all too much, cry *nimiety*.

Eelfare

Eelfare is not, as you might think, welfare for eels, but the passage of young eels up a river. Do they need their own word for it? It seems they do, since it is quite the phenomenon. The zoologist William Yarrell, born on this day in 1784, writes about it in his seminal two-volume *A History of British Fishes* (1836), noting the remarkable fact that in the spring of 1832, two observers counted 1,600–1,800 young eels, 'each about three inches long', passing up the Thames every single minute. That is a lot of eels.

Farrell explains, too, the term's derivation: 'This passage of young eels is called *Eel-fare* on the banks of the Thames, – the Saxon word [*faran*] signifying to go, to pass, to travel; and I have very little doubt that the word *Elver*, in common use on the banks of the Severn for a young eel, is a modification or corruption of *eel-fare*.' On this the *OED*, happily, agrees.

Mussitation

Listen – can you hear that low murmuring in the distance? Let's call it a *mussitation*. The word comes from the Latin for 'a subdued noise', originally as made specifically by dogs, but it was later applied to people too. The humming sound of *murmuring* is all very well, but sometimes you might want a word to express a sound with a bit more sibilance, as of people quietly saying prayers – and so the word *mussitation* was employed in 1649.

Most picturesquely, the English clergyman Arthur Young wrote in 1734 of 'the Murmur, or *Mussitation*, which Liquor makes that is pent up in a Bottle'. Dreaming, no doubt, of being released on such a day as this, celebrated in the US as National Cognac Day.

Boscage

The diplomat and writer Sir Henry Wotton, who began his studies at Cambridge on this day in 1584, is known for having coined the witticism 'An ambassador is an honest man sent to lie abroad for the commonwealth;' he is also the authority cited by Thomas Blount for the definition of *boscage*, in his 1624 book *Elements of Architecture*, where he describes where various sorts of art should be put in a house: 'Cheerful Paintings in Feasting and Banqueting Rooms, graver Stories in Galleries, Landscapes and *Boscage*, and such wild Works, in open Terraces or in summer Houses.'

From the Latin *boscum* ('wood'), *boscage* was adopted to mean both the genre of painting that featured forested land (or as the *OED* prettily puts it, 'sylvan scenery'), and also a thicket or grove of trees or shrubs. In 1730, Princess Wilhelmine of Prussia described how, as cited in Thomas Carlyle's English rendition in his *History of Friedrich II of Prussia* (1858–65) how 'we were all dancing in the fine saloons of Monbijou, with pretty intervals in the cool *boscages* and orangeries of the place'. So, then, a fine *boscage* might also do as a chill-out room for a party.

6 June

Antejentacular

Obviously nothing at all should happen before breakfast; but if it does, whatever horror it is can be termed *antejentacular*. It comes straight from the Latin for breakfast, *ientaculum*, and so *jentacular* itself is a comforting word, meaning, from 1721, 'of or belonging to breakfast'.

The unnatural *antejentacular*, by contrast, was coined by none other than the philosopher Jeremy Bentham, a prime theorist of utilitarianism, who died on this day in 1832. In a 1796 letter he confessed that he had had trouble sleeping because of toothache, and been forced to go on an '*antejentacular* walk muffled with two handkerchiefs'. It might after all have been a better idea to stay in bed.

Accismus

Human beings have not invented many new ways of being disingenuous over the last two millennia, as attested by the fact that the language of ancient rhetoric has so many specific terms for argumentative gambits. Pleasant to roll around the tongue is *accismus*, which means pretending to refuse something you actually really want. Cromwell's refusal of the crown was called *accismus* by some observers, and it is a polite form of *accismus*, too, if one responds 'Oh I couldn't possibly' when offered some luxurious morsel by one's host.

The word first appears in English in the great *Thesaurus* (1565) published by Thomas Cooper, Bishop of Winchester. (Cooper it was who first brought the word *thesaurus*, too, into the English language, from the Greek for 'treasury'; Shakespeare himself, it is thought, gladly used what became known as Cooper's Dictionary.) According to the later biographical sketch by John Aubrey in *Brief Lives*, Cooper's wife was so annoyed by his habit of staying up late working on his dictionary that one night she crept into his study and consigned half of it to the flames. 'Well,' Aubrey continues, 'for all that, that good man had so great a zeal for the advancement of learning, that he began it again.' Aubrey, the best and among the earliest biographers, was buried on this day in 1697.

Anonymuncule

One of the favourite pastimes of writers through the ages has been to dream up insults to hurl at other writers. Let us celebrate Algernon Swinburne doing just that, in a letter he wrote to a friend in 1867, complaining manfully about some nameless critic who had attacked his work. 'I have always found,' Swinburne wrote airily, 'that these "*anonymuncules*" vanish or collapse as soon as one attempts to set foot on them.'

Formed from *anonymous* and *homunculus* (Latin for 'little man'), this term for 'a petty anonymous writer' (*OED*) was in fact coined – 'so well and scientifically defined', as Swinburne noted – by the novelist and playwright Charles Reade, who was born on this day in 1814. It could as well be usefully employed today for nameless trolls on the internet.

Barmecide

In *The Thousand and One Nights*, the tale is told of a Prince Barmecide (in Arabic, *Barmaki*), who invites a beggar into his home and proceeds to 'feed' him a variety of lavishly described but entirely imaginary dishes, mouthfuls of air that the beggar pretends nonetheless to enjoy. So in English a *Barmecide* has come to mean a person who offers imaginary benefits, and *a Barmecide feast* means an insincere or illusory generosity.

This, you might think, is slightly unfair, since the original story has a happy ending. The beggar, pretending to be drunk on the imaginary liquor the Prince has served him, punches his host, and then, by way of an apology, says that he shouldn't have served him so much alcohol. The Prince bursts out laughing, and they become excellent friends. So Charles Dickens – who died on this day in 1870 – arguably used the term more justly: in his *American Notes* he wrote of Washington, DC, that it was 'a Barmecide Feast: a pleasant field for the imagination to rove in'.

Philippic

A savage criticism, attack, or take-down is a *philippic* (pronounced FYElippic), even though it should in all fairness be a *demosthenic*, since the term comes from two famous denunciations of Philip II of Macedon by the Greek statesman Demosthenes. In admiration, people later called Cicero's orations against Mark Antony *philippics* too, and the term has been handed down as indicating praise for particularly spectacular abuse.

The *philippic* is also one of the modes of address favoured by Prince Philip, Duke of Edinburgh, who was born on this day in 1921; at least according to the writer Alan Coren, who in 1988 reported thus: 'In one of his jollier fulminations, he drew a remarkable distinction anent [about] the manufacture of meat. The *philippic* pith was couched, admittedly, in an analogy about wives and prostitutes so convoluted as to leave even the smartest of structuralists crawling on all fours towards the nearest vodka, but his point, when it came, was needle-sharp. The world, according to the great consort, was split up into hunters and butchers: hunters did it for fun, butchers did it for money.'

11 JUNE

Addubitation

This sentence is an example of the kind of rhetorical – what shall I say? – flourish described by the fine word *addubitation*. When a speaker or writer asks a hesitant question in this way, it is not necessarily a *rhetorical question*, because a rhetorical question is one that strongly implies an (unspoken) answer. A question that serves to indicate contemplation or doubt is instead an example of *addubitation*, which is the rhetorical practice of appearing to be uncertain, or to debate with oneself.

It comes from the Latin *addubitatio*, meaning 'pretended hesitation or doubt' (*OED*), and first appears in its English form in a manual of literary devices called *The Arcadian Rhetoric*, which was entered into the Stationers' Register on this day in 1588. Its author, the poet and lawyer Abraham Fraunce, a close friend of Sir Philip Sidney, here writes: 'Deliberation is either in *Addubitation*, or communication. *Addubitation* or doubting is a kind of deliberation with our selves.' Modern politicians are so concerned to appear certain and knowledgeable that they are perhaps missing a trick of charm in not employing *addubitation* more often.

12 JUNE

Cark

If you are *carked* you are, literally, burdened, from the Latin *carricare*, 'to load' (whence also *charge*). But just as you can be burdened with sorrow as well as with a heavy bag, so since the fourteenth century to be *carked* has also meant, in particular, to be troubled or worried. In a medieval Arthurian romance, for example, it is said that after the enemy captured his castle, Cradelman, the king of North Wales, 'was sore *carked*', as well one might be.

One can also be said to *cark* (to worry or brood'), and this vivid verb survived in literary practice well into the nineteenth century. The novelist Charles Kingsley, born on this day in 1819, uses it in *Alton Locke* (1848), wherein the following political ditty is recorded: 'Down, down, down and down, / With idler, knave, and tyrant! / Why for sluggards *cark* and moil? / He that will not live by toil / Has no right on English soil! / God's word's our warrant!' Kingsley himself, a Christian socialist, was deeply concerned about rural poverty. That being a phenomenon not yet expunged from the Earth, one might still *cark* about it.

Meiosis

The first recorded appearance of *meiosis* is in the first English compendium of figures of speech, which gloried in the title *A Treatise of Schemes and Tropes very profitable for the better understanding of good authors, gathered out of the best Grammarians and Oratours by Richard Sherry Londoner* (1550). Therein we are told that it is a species of *Diminutio* or diminution, 'when great matters are made light of by words'. Since then *meiosis* has been the term for any kind of deliberate understatement, as when, after the end of the American Civil War, people in the South would refer to it as 'the recent unpleasantness'.

Sometimes meiosis is intended humorously, as a species of irony which also covers the phenomenon of *litotes* (see 3 December). In the 1934 novel *Busman's Honeymoon* by Dorothy L. Sayers – born on this day in 1893 – there is meanwhile a splendid application of the concept to matters other than the purely verbal. Lord Peter Wimsey pours 'a small quantity of sherry into a tumbler for his wife', who takes it with the remark: 'You are a master of *meiosis*.'

14 JUNE

Ullage

A glass-half-full person will concentrate on the quantity of the beverage remaining, whereas a glass-half-empty person will see only the – what? Space? Void? There is a word for precisely what is wanting, and that is *ullage*. In medieval times, a wine barrel or liquor cask would leak during transportation, and *ullage* – from the Old French *ouiller* ('to fill a barrel') – was the quantity required to fill it up again. By 1706, *ullage* could also mean the space left behind, or as a dictionary put it: '*Ullage* of a Cask, is what such a Vessel wants of being full.'

At length *ullage* ended up meaning both the half-full bit and the half-empty bit, as the *Encyclopaedia Britannica* explained: 'The quantity of liquor contained in a cask partially filled and the capacity of the portion which is empty are termed respectively the wet and dry *ullage*.' The English bibliophile John Camden Hotten, who died on this day in 1873, defined it thus in his *Dictionary of Modern Slang*: '*Ullages*, the wine of all sorts left in the bottoms of glasses at a public dinner' (i.e., dregs). And an 1867 sailor's dictionary noted that *ullage* could apply to solids as well as to liquids. After which, all one can do is nod sagely at the *ullage* of one's glass and hope someone offers to go to the bar.

15 JUNE

Pungitive

The British food and sports writer Peter Grove, who died on this day in 2016, was known as the 'curry legend' for his promotion of what became the national cuisine of the United Kingdom. *Pungitive* is a word tailor-made for the more adventurous kinds of such dishes: it means 'sharp', 'stinging', or 'cutting', from the Latin *pungitivus* ('piercing'). This is related to the more common word *pungent*, usually ascribed to smells or flavours – from Latin *pungus* ('piquant') – but *pungitive* has a stronger sense of biting or puncturing, and might be just what you need to describe an unexpectedly hot daal or kimchi.

A considerate author in 1484 advised readers to be aware of the kind of 'evil chewings' that were too *pungitive*, including mustard, garlic, and onions. (It was an age of more innocent palates.) The word, attested since 1425, need not describe only tastes, however: writers have described, for example, 'the *pungitive* prick of necessity' (1586), or 'a *pungitive* pain in the side' (1764).

16 JUNE

Quop

An invaluable word to know at Scrabble, *quop* means 'to wriggle, throb, or pulsate', as it is used of a slowly asphyxiating fish in the first recorded instance (spelled *quap*) in John Wycliffe's 1382 Bible. Later, in John Dryden's 1669 comedy *The Wild Gallant*, a tailor's wife, promised a place at court, exclaims: 'Oh how my heart *quops* now, as they say.' Where does such a strange word come from? It is, judges the *OED*, 'ultimately imitative', deriving from antecedents such as the Middle Dutch *quabbelen*, 'to quiver, wobble (originally used of fatty body parts of animals)'.

Today is Bloomsday, the date on which Leopold Bloom, the hero of *Ulysses*, goes on his voyage around Dublin. Could the great James Joyce ignore the existence of such a splendid word? He could not, and so in the novel we find the lovely line: 'His heart quopped softly.'

17 JUNE

Noctivagant

On this day in 1816, the writer John William Polidori confided to his diary: 'The ghost stories are begun by all but me.' The previous day, in the Swiss villa where they were all staying, Byron had suggested everyone write a tale of the supernatural. This challenge resulted most famously in Mary Shelley's *Frankenstein*, but also in Polidori's own creepy short story 'The Vampyre', which is the source of the modern vampire myth.

If you creep around during the hours of darkness like one of these undead creatures, you are *noctivagant*, from the Latin for 'night-wandering'. What other kind of creatures are *noctivagant*? According to the history of the word's usage, they are likely to be adulterers, students, or predatory animals.

One writer in the seventeenth century adds sternly: '*Noctivagants* are negligent in their habits.' This seems rather harsh today, since so many people – hospital staff, say, or fast-food delivery drivers – are *noctivagant* by necessity, while others are hard at work on their *lucubrations* (see 22 January), and yet others simply enjoy the peace of the dark hours. The *noctivagants* of the world see it differently, and who is to say not more accurately?

18 JUNE

Discountenancer

A person who habitually raises an eyebrow, or sneers, at the actions of others, is a *discountenancer*, one who expresses disapproval. It comes from the Latin *continentia* ('comportment'), which in the English version, *countenance*, comes to mean 'face'. As Dr Johnson has it, a discountenancer is 'One that discourages by cold treatment; one that depresses by unfriendly regard'.

But you don't need to use your face to be a *discountenancer*; it can, usefully, also be done in words, or perhaps through divine intervention in judicial proceedings. The radical writer William Cobbett, who died on this day in 1835, writes in his *Parliamentary History of England* (1806) that the maxim 'The supreme law is the good of the people' should not encourage law-breaking, and that God himself is 'a *discountenancer* thereof, even where it hath been with good intentions'.

Boutefeu

Of this word, Thomas Blount writes: 'The literal signification is one that blows the fire, or that wilfully sets houses on fire; but Metaphorically it is used for one that raiseth discord, an Incendiary, a fire-brand of Sedition, one that loves to set and see men at strife.' From the French *bouter* ('to put') and *feu* ('fire'), *boutefeu* was originally a political rebel of the sort that wanted to see oppressive tradition burn, such as the French revolutionaries who, on this day in 1790, issued a decree abolishing the titles and privileges of the nobility.

More generally, our lusts could be described as *boutefeus*, and so even could some publishers. The novelist Samuel Richardson said of some lately distributed tracts that 'the Sale is far from answering the sanguine Expectations of their *Boutefeu* Editor'. Such a person, we may assume, is one who publishes in order to sow controversy and discord. The modern age might be remarkable in knowing the greatest number of *boutefeu* editors yet seen.

20 June

Resistentialism

Have you ever suspected that inanimate objects are conspiring against you? You are not alone. '*Les choses sont contre nous*' ('Things are against us') is the slogan of fellow sufferers, according to the English humorist Paul Jennings, who was born on this day in 1918 and coined the name of this philosophy, *resistentialism*, in a 1948 column for the *Spectator*. Previous philosophies, he said, 'were concerned merely with what men think about Things. Now *resistentialism* is the philosophy of what Things think about us.'

Jennings mentions, as examples, the scientific finding that marmalade on toast, when dropped, was found to be much more likely to fall face-down if there was an expensive carpet beneath; and 'thousands of experiments in which subjects of all ages and sexes, sitting in chairs of every conceivable kind, dropped various kinds of pencil. In only three cases did the pencil come to rest within easy reach.' Existentialism is challenging, but only the truly courageous can embrace *resistentialism*.

21 JUNE

Prickmedainty

In 1529 the English poet John Skelton – who died on this day in 1529 – wrote: 'There was a *pryckemedenty*, / Sat lyke a seynty, / And began to paynty, / As thoughe she would faynty.' A 'seynty' is a saint, and 'paynty' is to paint – i.e. (in this context) to feign. But the main word of interest here is the marvellous *pryckemedenty*, later spelled more recognizably as *prickmedainty*, which describes anyone over-concerned with their appearance.

Why 'prick'? It comes from that sense of the word used to mean 'to dress up elaborately' (in garments fastened with many pins, and so forth). So a *prickmedainty* is a person affectedly dressed, dandyish, or narcissistic, and the word may also be used adjectivally, as in that person's *prickmedainty* obsession with taking selfies.

22 JUNE

Moky

Those living at northerly latitudes have good reason to invent many words for unpleasant weather: one such near-forgotten gem is *moky*. Dr Johnson defines it thus: 'Dark; as moky weather. It seems a corruption of murky: and in some places they call it muggy, dusky.' The *OED* agrees that there is a possible relation to *muggy*, and also points to *moch*, an old Germanic word meaning 'humid'.

The writer George Hardinge, born on this day in 1743, composed a satirical dialogue, *Rowley and Chatterton in the Shades* (1782), about the supposed fifteenth-century monk called Thomas Rowley, whose poems had lately been 'discovered' and published. (Hardinge was among those who correctly supposed that they were in fact the work of Thomas Chatterton.) In the satire, the ghost of Chatterton attempts to prove to the ghost of Rowley that he is, indeed, English: 'Yes, Sir, I was born in that part of the world ... "*mokie*" clouds "honge" over the "londe", and Englonde lies "smeethynge" with a "lethal wounde"; "roin and sleeter" prevail ...' Rowley immediately recognizes this as a Somersetshire accent. In our time, whenever the weather is dark with cloud, inhabitants of Lincolnshire might still call it a *moky* old day; but why should they have all the fun?

Lurdan

Should one need to express particular *contumely* (see 27 July) for a dull sluggardly rascal, there is the very old word *lurdan*, from the French *lourd* ('heavy'). In *Of Reformation* (1641), John Milton addresses an anthropomorphized tumour, representing the bishops, thus: '*Lourdan*, quoth the Philosopher, thy folly is as great as thy filth.' It can also work adjectivally: others have been energetically abused as 'lazy *lurdan* Friars', '*lurdane* knights', and so forth.

One should be careful to remember that *lurdans* are not harmless. On this day in 1314 began the Battle of Bannockburn, which ended in Robert the Bruce's victory over Edward II's English forces. It is vividly described in a verse chronicle, *The Bruce* (1375), by John Barbour, who also describes the earlier siege of Kildrummy Castle, defended by Robert's brother. In that battle the defenders fell because 'There within was a traitor, a false *lurdane*, one losenger [deceiver]': their blacksmith, Osbourne, betrayed his side and set the castle on fire.

24 JUNE

Incompossible

When you want to say as forcefully as you can that two things are incompatible, or contradictory, you want the old word *incompossible*. It is first recorded in 1605, when a writer points out that clerical rule by the Roman church is *incompossible* with the supremacy of princes. The two make a logical contradiction: they cannot both exist in the same world.

The great American satirist Ambrose Bierce, born on this day in 1842, provides an excellent illustration of the meaning of *incompossible* in his *Devil's Dictionary*. 'Two things are *incompossible*,' he writes, 'when the world of being has scope enough for one of them, but not enough for both – as Walt Whitman's poetry and God's mercy to man.'

25 JUNE

Misling

The American philosopher Willard Van Orman Quine was born on this date in 1908, and worked in Naval Intelligence during the Second World War. In his 1987 book *Quiddities: An Intermittently Philosophical Dictionary*, he proposes a new word for the very old concept of deceiving people without actually lying. This, Quine suggests, we should call *misling*. Why *misling*? Because it is common to misread 'misled' as sounding like 'mizzled', and on that basis the participle would indeed be *misling*, instead of 'misleading'.

The philosopher was apparently unaware that *misling* already existed, once being an alternate spelling of *maslin*, a mixture of different types of grain. But we could still profit from his proposed use of it as 'a mild word for the restrained sort of deception, not quite actionable as fraud even in Ralph Nader's day, that has a respected place in enlightened modern advertising'. One ingenious fish entrepreneur, Quine relates, had the problem that his tinned salmon was anaemically white, rather than the fresh pink colour it ought to have been. So he emblazoned the product with the slogan 'Guaranteed not to turn red in the can'. Modern readers will surely not be short of further examples.

Haecceity

How do you describe the dogness of your dog, or the rock-ness of that rock? You want the hard-to-spell but beautiful word *haecceity* (pronounced hikeEYity). It was introduced by the thirteenth-century philosopher Duns Scotus, in a Latin form derived from *haec*, the feminine of *hoc*, meaning, simply, 'this'. So *haecceity* is 'thisness'; or, as the *OED* puts it: 'The quality that makes a person or thing describable as "this"; the property of being a unique and individual thing; particular character, individuality.' This is not to be confused with *quiddity*, from the Latin *quid* ('that'), for an intrinsic nature or essence. Your dog's *quiddity* makes him an example of the species *Canis familiaris*, but his *haecceity* is in the particular way he wags his tail.

Not everyone, it is fair to say, has seen the need for such terms. The clergyman and philosopher Ralph Cudworth, who died on this day in 1688, expostulated thus: 'Scholastics ... could not make a Rational Discourse of any thing ... but they must stuff it with their Quiddities, Entities, Essences, *Hæcceities*, and the like.' This he wrote in a book entitled *The True Intellectual System of the Universe* (1678): a wonderfully vainglorious title that definitely has its own tangy *haecceity*.

27 JUNE

Teratology

From the Greek, it looks as though *teratology* ought to mean the study of monsters: *teras* ('monster'), plus *logos* ('word' or 'study'). But *teras* also means 'prodigy' or 'marvel', or more neutrally 'something misshapen or ill-formed': a *teratoma* in medicine is a tumour composed of different bodily tissues, and *teratology* in biology more generally is the study of abnormal formations.

In literature, however, *teratology* is specifically an emphasis upon the fantastical. *An Universal Etymological English Dictionary* (1721) by the philologist Nathan Bailey – who died on this day in 1742 – defines it thus: '*Teratology* ... is when bold Writers, fond of the sublime, intermix something great and prodigious in every Thing they write, whether there be Foundation for it in Reason or not, and this is what is call'd Bombast.' Twenty-first-century entertainment being mainly about wizards, mutants, aliens, and so forth, we might call it a whole culture of *teratology*.

Paraph

The *paraph* is the flourish or squiggle made after or underneath a signature, originally as an anti-forgery precaution. It is explained thus in Blount's *Glossographia* (1656): 'the flourish or peculiar knot or mark set unto, after, or instead of, a name in the signing a Deed or Letter, and generally any such graceful setting out of a man's hand or name in writing'. The signature of the scientist and statesman Francis Bacon, for example, had for its *paraph*, as a later writer explained, 'a loop-headed triangle, with a lozenge below'. And the signature of Henry VIII, who was born on this day in 1491, has for a paraph an elaborate R, signifying 'King' (Latin *Rex*).

Perhaps confusingly, *paraph* shares its root with *paragraph* (the Greek literally means 'around writing'), and has sometimes been used to mean 'paragraph' or the paragraph mark, the pilcrow: ¶. But the specialized sense is more fun. In her *Sexual Deviations As Seen in Handwriting* (1990), the author Marie Bernard, a German-born practitioner of the doubtful art of graphology, cites a fellow expert's analysis of a signature thus: 'Discordancy of form between the two *paraphs*, discordancy of pressure in the pressure of the last *paraph*.' If you do not wish your secret desires to be revealed, better be careful where you leave your signature.

Imaginarian

An *imaginarian* is someone primarily concerned with imaginary things. When it first appeared in 1729, it was used negatively, to mean 'a fantasist'. The American minister and poet of the 'American baroque', Edward Taylor, who died on this day in 1729, employed the word in a long poem (posthumously given the rather offputting title *A Metrical History of Christianity*) to describe Constantine's opinion of the Byzantine emperor Nicephorus as a 'vain *Imaginarian*'.

Of late, though, the title of *imaginarian* has been reclaimed as a badge of pride, maybe because the real world as it is seems increasingly crass and toxic, and perhaps also owing to the relatively positive associations of the noun-phrase *the imaginary* in psychoanalysis, sociology, and literary theory. So the female hip-hop/pop band Northern State described themselves in 'A Thousand Words' (2002) as follows: 'I'm a vegetarian, humanitarian, *imaginarian*, not a libertarian.'

30 JUNE

Psithurism

The British physicist Lord Rayleigh, who died on this day in 1919, counted among his achievements the discovery of what he called 'whispering-gallery waves': sound waves that can travel along a concave surface and so create the famous effect of the Whispering Gallery under the dome in St Paul's Cathedral, where the quietest whisper may be heard from the opposite side.

If you experience this effect you may say that you are hearing *psithurism*, a poetic word for 'whispering'. It comes straight from the Greek word *psithurisma* – itself no doubt onomatopoeic – which was introduced to anglophone readers by the Romantic writer Leigh Hunt, when speaking of Greek pastoral poetry: 'The Greek word for rustling, or rather whispering – *psithurisma* – is much admired. "Whispering" is hardly strong enough, and not so long drawn out. There is the continuous whisper in *psithurisma*.' The word was later Englished to *psithurism*, and patiently awaits anyone who cares to say it, very softly.

JULY

1 July

Bedpresser

One of those old compound terms that is almost a picto-gram of the thing it describes, *bedpresser* denotes, according to Dr Johnson, 'a heavy lazy fellow'. In Shakespeare's *Henry IV, Part 1*, Hal and Falstaff have a spectacular exchange of insults, with the former calling the latter 'this *bed-presser*, this horseback-breaker, this huge hill of flesh'. In his *Essays* of 1600, meanwhile, Sir William Cornwallis – who was buried on this day in 1614 – warned: 'Fame never yet knew a per-petual *bedpresser*.' Have a lie-in in his memory.

Alfear

The Russian-American novelist Vladimir Nabokov died on this day in 1977. Among his most spectacular achievements is the novel *Pale Fire* (1962). Here, in Charles Kinbote's notes to John Shade's titular poem, the King of Zembla is heading towards a mountain pass, when: 'A shiver of *alfear* (uncontrollable fear caused by elves) ran between his shoulder-blades.'

The word *alfear* (perhaps related to the Icelandic *alfur*, 'elf') is, I regret to report, attested nowhere else, and so breaks this book's general rule against nonce-words, but it is too good not to include. It is very possibly the condition experienced by the scholar Hugo Dyson, who was among the friends to whom J. R. R. Tolkien used to read instalments of *The Lord of the Rings*. On one such occasion, Dyson is said to have muttered: 'Oh fuck, not another elf.'

Aposiopesis

In one of his autobiographical sketches, published in this month in 1845, Thomas De Quincey relates how, at school, the headmaster would annoy the older boys by constantly mentioning how brilliant the young De Quincey's poems were compared to their own. At length the boys had had enough. One of them came up to De Quincey and punched him on the shoulder, asking what the devil he meant by being so brilliant. 'I was briefly admonished,' De Quincey relates, 'to see that I wrote worse for the future, or else——.' Or else what? The speaker trailed off. 'At this *aposiopesis* I looked inquiringly at the speaker,' De Quincey continues, 'and he filled up the chasm by saying, that he would "annihilate" me.'

An *aposiopesis* ('or else ...') – from the Greek *aposiopan* ('to keep silent') – is a halt in speech for rhetorical effect. Alexander Pope calls it 'an excellent Figure for the Ignorant, as, *What shall I say?* when one has nothing to say; or *I can no more*, when one really can no more'. The reader will surely agree that I need hardly add further explanation.

Compotation

This being Independence Day in the US, it offers a fine excuse for lovers of liberty and other Americans to join in an amicable *compotation*, which is a convivial old word for 'having a drink together' (Latin *com–*, 'with', plus *potare*, 'to drink'). Whereas at a *symposium* (which is Greek for the same thing), you might feel expected to philosophize, endure fine dining, or deliver a dreary conference paper, a *compotation* is a simple 'drinking-bout' or 'carouse' (*OED*).

In a sixteenth-century comic tale called *Bacchus' Bountie*, we learn of one man's ingenious method of avoiding a hangover: 'with him he brought a nightcap for god Bacchus' great godhead, lest, through his hot *compotations* in the day, his head should crow with cold consumptions in the night'. Perhaps not guaranteed to be effective, but worth a try.

Crapulent

A *crapulent* person is one devoted – as, perhaps, last night – to the worship of Bacchus, or, as Ambrose Bierce defines the word: 'As gentlemen wish to be who love their landlords – otherwise barkeepers.' To put it more directly, to be *crapulent* is to be suffering the after-effects of a debauch, following excessive eating or drinking, or both. The jazz musician George Melly, who died on this day in 2007, used the music of Bessie Smith to ameliorate this state: 'I still play Bessie's songs every day. I have all her tapes. I play two of them while I'm getting dressed, or three if I've got a hangover.'

One might suspect here an association with the word *crap*, but there seems none: *crap* is probably from the Latin *crappa* (the rubbish to be found on the floor of a barn); while *crapulent* derives from *kraipale*, the Greek for 'hung-over nausea'. It need not only be used, of course, literally for that morning-after feeling; a nineteenth-century writer, for example, recalls a time 'When the collective wisdom of the country was in an intensely *crapulent* state'. Many more such times were to follow.

Rodomontade

An epic outbreak of bombastic boastfulness is a *rodomontade*. In 1711, the Earl of Shaftesbury railed against 'the incorrigibleness of our poets, in their pedantic manner, their vanity, their defiance of criticism, their *rhodomontade*, and poetical bravado'. (He had a particular grudge against Dryden, who had painted Shaftesbury's grandfather in an unflattering satirical light.) Later, William Hazlitt had had it up to here with the writing of show-off theatre critics: 'Not a glimpse can you get of the merits or defects of the performers: they are hidden in a profusion of barbarous epithets and wilful *rhodomontade*.'

As those examples suggest, the word has sometimes been spelled with an *h*, though it has nothing to do with the roots of *rhododendron* (literally 'rose tree'). *Rodomontade* is actually an eponym, formed from the name of the character Rodomonte, the quick-tempered and vainglorious Saracen leader in the epic poem *Orlando Innamorato* by Boiardo (1495). Rodomonte appears, too, in its more famous sequel, *Orlando Furioso* (1532), which was effectively fan-fiction by a different author: the great Ludovico Ariosto, who is credited with coining the term *humanism* – and died on this day in 1533.

Velleity

Today is World Chocolate Day, but if you quite fancy some chocolate but can't be bothered to get up and look for some, you can rhetorically ennoble your lassitude with the pretty word *velleity*: 'The fact or quality of merely willing, wishing, or desiring, without any effort or advance towards action or realization' (*OED*).

In his 1640 book *A Treatise of the Passions and Faculties of the Soule of Man*, the clergyman Edward Reynolds warned that desires for something which hoped to escape the labour or pains of acquiring it were useless: 'They are only *Velleities* and not Volitions: half and broken wishes, not whole desires, which are not industrious; but away in sluggish and empty speculations. Fisherman that will take the Fish, must be contented to be dashed with the Water. And he that will expect to have his desires answered, must put as well his hands as his prayers unto them.'

8 July

Empleomania

Someone who has a perverse desire or mania for holding public office is suffering from *empleomania*. The word comes from the Spanish *empleo* ('job'), plus *mania*, and is first recorded in English as used by snooty writers looking down on the politics of Spain in the nineteenth century. Of the Spanish prime minister Luis González-Bravo y López de Arjona, the British writer T. M. Hughes – himself an immigrant to Spain – sneered in 1845: 'This first of prime ministers is the living impersonation and type of the prevailing Spanish vice of *empleomania*, or rage for office.'

In fact, Luis González-Bravo, who was born on this day in 1811, was considered a fine orator, and was also a writer, a founder of newspapers, and a patron of the arts. Better, perhaps, to reserve the term *empleomania* for modern politicians who do nothing else with their lives but seek power.

Scrouge

To *scrouge* someone (sometimes spelled *scrooge*) is 'to incommode by pressing against (a person); to encroach on (a person's) space in sitting or standing; to crowd', says the OED, suggesting that it is a variant of *scruze*, a combination of *screw* and *squeeze*. It can also simply mean to squeeze or rummage. In *The Wind in the Willows* by Kenneth Grahame, who was buried on this day in 1932, Mole decides he has had enough of spring-cleaning and wants to tunnel up to the surface. 'So he scraped and scratched and scrabbled and *scrooged* and then he *scrooged* again and scrabbled and scratched and scraped, working busily with his little paws and muttering to himself, "Up we go! Up we go!" till at last, pop! his snout came out into the sunlight, and he found himself rolling in the warm grass of a great meadow.'

In its transitive use, to mean bothering people by coming too close to them, *scrouge* is of surprisingly old vintage. Dr Johnson calls it 'London jargon' in 1755. London not having become any less crowded since then, *scrouge* is a good word for the experience of travelling around it, or on the New York subway. In an 1811 novel by Amelia Beauclerc, a young man asks a woman: 'I hope, Miss, I don't *scrouge* you?' Today's manspreaders, alas, are not so considerate.

Minimifidian

The *minimifidian* is that pragmatic person who has the absolute least necessary belief in anything at all to get by (from the Latin for 'minimum faith'). In the form *minimifidianism*, the word was coined by Samuel Taylor Coleridge, in his *Aids to Reflection* (1825). Says he: 'Sir Thomas Browne, in his *Religio Medici*, complains, that there are not impossibilities enough in Religion for his active faith; and adopts by choice ... such interpretations of ... Holy Writ, as place them in irreconcilable contradiction to the demonstrations of science ... because (says he) "I love to lose myself in a mystery."' This impressive attitude Coleridge dubs *ultrafidianism* – maximum belief. (Thomas Browne, let it be remembered, was also a fine naturalist and all-round polymath, having received his Doctor of Medicine degree from Oxford on this day in 1637.)

By contrast, Coleridge continues, 'there is a scheme constructed on the principle of retaining the social sympathies, that attend on the name of Believer, at the least possible expenditure of Belief'. And this he calls *minimifidianism*. Coleridge does not approve of either of these – what he calls 'extremes' – but in our day it may be found that the latter is more conducive to good cheer and the harmony of humankind.

11 July

Firk

To *firk* is to make any one of a number of sudden, sharp motions: in medieval times you could *firk* someone's head off, *firk* them (wake them up), or *firk* them to death. The diplomat and natural philosopher Kenelm Digby, born on this day in 1603, used the term to describe vulpine behaviour: when being chased by dogs, he writes, a fox 'will piss upon his tail, and by *firking* that up and down, will endeavour (you may believe) to make their eyes smart, and so retard their pursuit, that he may escape from them'. Clever fox.

If the sound of the word *firk* tempts you to snigger, you are not alone; it seems likely that Ben Jonson deliberately invited such sniggers in his 1610 play *The Alchemist*, when Sir Epicure Mammon comments: 'That's his fire-drake, / His lungs, his Zephyrus, he that puffs his coals, / Till he *firk* nature up, in her own centre.' *Firking* nature up is not something we have since ceased from doing.

Mumpsimus

A custom or notion that has been shown to be unreasonable but nonetheless persists is a *mumpsimus*. Splendidly, this word is an example of what it refers to. As told by the great Renaissance scholar Erasmus, who died on this day in 1536, the story goes that once upon a time, an illiterate English priest was scolded for having read '*quod ore mumpsimus*' in the Latin Mass when he should have said *sumpsimus* ('we have taken'). The priest replied heroically: 'I will not change my old *mumpsimus* for your new sumpsimus.'

And so *mumpsimus* is a wrong but still-current idea, or the kind of person who sticks to it. *Mumpsimus* held its currency well into the twentieth century; in this age of renewed Flat Earthism and anti-vaccine propaganda, perhaps it needs vigorous use once more.

Tellurian

Geologists rejoice, for today is International Rock Day, and so among the most *tellurian* of celebrations. In classical Latin, *Tellus* is the Earth, and also the goddess of the Earth, a kind of sister to sea-god Neptune, as the Player King mentions them in *Hamlet*: 'Full thirty times hath Phoebus' cart gone round / Neptune's salt wash, and Tellus' orbèd ground.' So, then, a *Tellurian* in eighteenth-century science was a mechanical model of the Earth's rotation, and *tellurian* was subsequently adopted as an adjective meaning simply 'of or about the Earth'.

Most usefully, *Ttellurian* was adopted by writers of science fiction to mean inhabitants of the planet in question, i.e. human beings, and was often so used well into the twentieth century: perhaps because it sounds both more noble than *Earthlings*, and more exotic than *Terrans*. The first recorded such use is in a translation of Aristophanes' comedy *Peace*, reviewed with excerpts in *Blackwood's* in 1828, where the Man in the Moon tells a visitor: 'Away, Tellurian!' Soon afterwards, Thomas De Quincey adopted the same nomenclature in his essay 'Joan of Arc', when he hypothesized about 'any distant worlds (which *may* be the case)' being 'so far ahead of us *Tellurians* in optical resources, as to see distinctly through their telescopes all that we do on Earth'. Look up now and wave to them, just in case.

Chrestomathic

A person who is *chrestomathic* is someone 'devoted to the learning of useful matters' (*OED*). The term entered English thanks to the publication of *Chrestomathia* (1817), a reformist plan for secondary-school education published by the philosopher Jeremy Bentham. His vision for a '*chrestomathic* school' included the abolition of corporal punishment, the use of visual aids, the centrality of science (rather than Latin and Greek), and the training of pupils in book-keeping as well as academic subjects.

Less rigorously, a *chrestomathy* (a collection of 'useful learning') is a sort of commonplace book, a compendium of passages from one or more writers, especially (but not exclusively) in order to assist with learning a language; or even, perhaps, a book such as this one. It was employed metaphorically by an admiring reviewer of the travel writing of the celebrated Parisian woman of letters and *grande salonnière* Madame de Staël, who died on this day in 1817. She, a reviewer for *Fraser's Magazine* later wrote, had embarked on her journeys 'to read the living book of man, as written in various tongues; nay, to read the *chrestomathy* and diamond edition of that living polyglot book of man'.

Logocentrism

The French philosopher Jacques Derrida, prince of deconstruction, was born on this day, in Algeria, in 1930. One of his most useful concepts is that of *logocentrism* (in the original French, *logocentrisme*). This is the dubious assumption, which Derrida finds to be central in Western thought, that speech (*logos*, the Greek for 'word') is more direct and authentic — somehow, closer to reality — than written language. (Derrida was not the first to use the word: the German philosopher Ludwig Klages coined the German equivalent, *das Logozentrisch*, in 1929; while *logocentric* to mean 'centred on reason' is attested in English from 1939.)

Derrida's multitudinous subsequent acolytes and interpreters have run with the term *logocentrism* in various different directions, but the basic insight is valuable; it explains, for example, why live political debates are still widely supposed to be the fundamental contests of democracy, unenlightening though they usually prove.

16 JULY

Tergiversation

This is a satisfying term, once one has learned how to pronounce it (TERdgiversation), of disapproval for shiftiness or evasiveness. It comes from the Latin *tergum* ('back'), plus *vertere* ('to turn'), so it was first used in English to mean turning one's back on one's cause, or party, or duties; then, 'turning away from straightforward or honest action'; and so 'shifting, shuffling, equivocation, prevarication' (*OED*).

The funeral of John Bramhall, philosopher and Archbishop of Armagh, was held on this day in 1663: he had argued, according to Dr Johnson, that 'Writing is to be preferred before verbal conferences, as being freer from passions and *tergiversations.*' In an ideal world it would be.

17 July

Cautelous

In Shakespeare's *Coriolanus*, the proud war-hero protagonist tells his mother: 'though I go alone, / Like to a lonely dragon that his fen / Makes fear'd and talk'd of more than seen, your son / Will or exceed the common or be caught / With *cautelous* baits and practice.' What is *cautelous* is wily and cunning, and perhaps here with a sense of underhandedness. From the Latin *cautela* ('precaution'), it has been said to be characteristic of the fox, the snake, and other much-slandered animals, as well as by Robert Browning of Barbarossa, the Holy Roman Emperor Frederick I.

But to be *cautelous* may also mean to be wise: it can have the meaning of 'circumspect' or 'heedful', as it would have served Coriolanus himself to be. Reviewing Peter Hall's production, starring Laurence Olivier, on this day in 1959, a reviewer wrote: '*Coriolanus* is a mature, alive, real play – more contemporary today than it would ever have been to the Elizabethans [sic: it was first performed in 1609 or 1610] or the Romans.' And arguably still more so now.

Morganatic

In his novel *The Luck of Barry Lyndon*, William Makepeace Thackeray, who was born on this day in 1811, has his narrator plot to marry a rich young princess, which might be achieved if the old duke and his wife agree: 'Her Highness had only to press the match upon the old Duke, over whom her influence was unbounded, and to secure the goodwill of the Countess of Liliengarten, (which was the romantic title of his Highness's morganatic spouse).' A *morganatic* husband or wife is one of lower status than their partner; and a *morganatic* marriage is one unequal in this way. The term derives from the Latin *morganaticum*, which means 'a morning gift'. Traditionally, a husband would present such a morning gift of property to his wife on the first day of their wedded life, but in a *morganatic* marriage she (and any children) would be entitled to no further share of his wealth or title.

In the late nineteenth century, Ambrose Bierce observed: '*Morganatic*: Pertaining to a kind of marriage between a man of exalted rank and a woman of low degree by which the wife gets nothing but a husband, and not much of a husband.' He added, further, the following fanciful etymology which time has not yet rendered obscure: 'From Morgan (J. P.), a kind of finance, by a transaction with whom nobody gets anything at all.'

19 July

Feriation

When, in Homer's *Iliad*, Achilles approaches Troy to fight Hector, we learn that Sirius, aka the Dog Star, has returned with all its evil portent. So commence what we now call the 'dog days' of summer – which began, according to one modern scholar's astronomical calculations, on this very day during the Trojan War itself. The oppressive heat of the season in the northern hemisphere has historically been associated with lassitude, and in modern times even trading on Wall Street still quietens down. For those people lucky enough to wind down their labours, or actually take a vacation, this is a traditional period of *feriation*.

A word for 'quietness, idleness' (Thomas Blount), or 'cessation of work' (*OED*), with as grand a sound as *feriation*, is, surely, to be treasured. (It comes from *feria*, the Latin for 'holiday'.) Indeed, since there is no commonly used English word that portrays the act of not working in a positive light, we should revive this one, and the associated verb, to *feriate*.

Discalceation

If you want to refer to taking off your shoes, but 'taking off my shoes' seems like a bit of a mouthful, you need the word *discalceation* (pronounced disκALκiation): 'the act of pulling off the shoes' (Dr Johnson), 'esp. as a token of reverence or humility' (*OED*). A seventeenth-century writer referred to 'The Pythagorean mode of *discalceation*, or putting off the shoes, at entrance into the Temple', while Johnson cites an authority on how *discalceation* at mealtimes was a method of keeping one's bed clean, for eating in bed was quite normal.

This might seem so rare a word that it's hardly worth mentioning, but a form of it does make a surprising appearance in the *caliginous* (see 10 November), post-apocalyptic novel *The Road* by Cormac McCarthy, who was born on this day in 1933. In it, the father and son come across some dead people: 'They were *discalced* to a man like pilgrims of some common order for all their shoes were long since stolen.' Could the unfortunate corpses really be said to have made an act of *discalceation* if their shoes had just been post-humously thieved by looters? It is a literary mystery for future scholars to ponder.

21 JULY

Prisage

James Butler, Duke of Ormond and latterly Lord Lieutenant of Ireland, who died on this day in 1688, was a fortunate fellow, not least in the cut he made from the wine trade. As his biographer later wrote, 'The Marquis did not esteem any part of his revenue so much, as he did that which arose from the *prisage* of wines ... every ship laden with wine that broke bulk in Ireland, paying him out of eighteen tun, two tun, one behind the mast and the other before.' (A *tun* was a large vat containing 240–250 gallons of wine.)

The *prisage* – from the French *prise*, past participle of *prendre*, to take or seize – was an ancient custom of payment in kind owed by native traders to the crown, or to persons appointed by the crown. Foreign traders, by contrast, would pay a similar toll but in *butlerage* (as a butler was an high-ranking official at court), and so the common phrase for such duties was *prisage and butlerage*. These practices were abolished in 1809, but governments around the world still levy duties on the sale of alcohol, and so, though its bene-fits might eventually be more democractially spread-out, *prisage* lives on.

Wanwit

Human beings have always needed words to describe their fellows as idiots, and *wanwit* is the English (chiefly Scottish) version of a long line that includes Old Icelandic *vanvit* ('lack of thought'), Old Swedish *vanvit* ('foolishness'), and Old Danish *wanwit* (ditto). The old prefix *wan–* is a negation (like *un–*), and survived in some English dialects in words such as *wancanny* and *wanfortunate*. The sense is more obvious in the alternative spelling *wantwit*, as used in Shakespeare's *The Merchant of Venice*, which was entered in the Stationers' Register on this day in 1598. Declares Antonio: 'And such a *want-wit* sadness makes of me, / That I have much ado to know myself.'

As well as the state of foolishness, *wanwit* can be usefully applied to the foolish person, as the Scottish chronicler Andrew Crawfurd recorded in his nineteenth-century saga of local life, *Cairn of Lochwinnoch*: 'Her brother David was rather a *wanwit* or sillie-daft man.' They remain omnipresent.

Eximious

If you want to call something *excellent* but fear that word is degraded through overuse, you might instead choose the lustrous alternative *eximious*, from the Latin *eximius*, meaning 'excepted' (and so 'exceptional'). Seventeenth-century apothecaries would sell you a syrup claimed to be '*eximious* against many affections', while heroic or just aristocratic persons of later ages were also routinely called *eximious*.

Of course, what seems *eximious* will depend on the context. In her 1960 novel *The Great Fortune*, Olivia Manning – who died on this day in 1980 – describes an English couple in Romania at the outbreak of the Second World War, who are delighted to find somewhere that still sells 'imports from England: Quaker Oats, tinned fruits, corned beef, Oxford marmalade – expensive luxuries *eximious* among luxury'.

Antimetabole

Alexandre Dumas was born on this day in 1802, and the deathless motto of his three musketeers – *Un pour tous, tous pour un*, or 'All for one, and one for all' – is an excellent example of the literary device of *antimetabole*. This is a reversal of the order of words in successive phrases. 'Ask not what your country can do for you,' said JFK, 'ask what you can do for your country.' Sherlock Holmes, meanwhile, had counselled against the temptation to 'twist facts to suit theories, instead of theories to suit facts'.

From the Greek *anti–* ('in the opposite direction') and *metabole* ('change' or 'turn about', from which we also get *metabolism*), *antimetabole* is a species of the device chiasmus (Greek for 'crossing'), which can also describe more generally any kind of grammatical inversion. In any case it is an excellent way to concoct memorable phrases, or, if you will, to phrase memorable concoctions.

25 JULY

Ipsedixitism

Someone who appeals to an idea he thinks is obvious and needs no further explanation is one given to the annoying habit of *ipsedixitism*. *Ipse dixit* is the Latin for 'the thing speaks for itself', but as we know, very little speaks for itself, and claiming that it does is very often a way to avoid being drawn into forensic criticism of one's position.

The vice of *ipsedixitism* was first named by the philosopher Jeremy Bentham around 1832, but Samuel Taylor Coleridge – who died on this day in 1834 – had anticipated the usage when speaking, in an 1808 letter to Humphry Davy, of the Introduction to Robert Southey's *Chronicle of the Cid*, which he found 'shallow, flippant, and *ipse dixitish*'. Happily – and unusually – Coleridge went on to say he thought the rest of the book quite excellent, not being one to cleave to rivalrous prejudices. 'It delights me to be able to speak thus of a work of Southey's,' he wrote. 'I am so often forced to quarrel with his want of Judgment and his Unthinkingness – which, heaven knows, I never do without pain & the vexation of a disappointed Wish.' A master, as of much else, of the backhanded compliment.

Absquatulate

From some dull party you might slip out, take a French leave, or say an Irish goodbye, but why not go the whole hog and say you will *absquatulate*. The word is first recorded in 1830 as *obsquatulate*, defined as 'to mosey, to abscond', but *absquatulate* became the preferred form thereafter. (The *OED* calls it a humorous formation from *ab-* and *squat*.)

Kurt Vonnegut writes in *Hocus Pocus* (1990) of 'some overthrown Caribbean or African dictator who had *absquatulated* to the USA with his starving nation's treasury', but the term is not exclusively American slang. It was employed for its comic effect, for example, by none other than George Bernard Shaw, born on this day in 1856. In *Fanny's First Play*, a young woman who wishes to escape an awkward situation says, 'Let me *absquatulate*,' and makes for the door. Juggins, the butler, replies: 'If you wish to leave without being seen, you had better step into my pantry and leave afterwards.' Literary butlers are full of sage advice.

Contumely

The worst possible sort of contemptuous, scornful, or insulting behaviour is *contumely* (from the Latin for 'abuse'), and is, in literature, something that must be stoically borne. Hamlet himself mentions 'the proud man's *contumely*' as one of the things that makes life not worth living. The word can also be used for an instance of such abuse: in George Chapman's 1615 version of Homer's *Odyssey*, for instance, Telemachus complains of the suitors milling around his mother at home. 'And would to god the gods would favour me ... that my injury / Done by my mother's wooers, being so foul, / I might revenge upon their every soul; / Who, pressing me with *contumelies*, dare / Such things as past the power of utt'rance are.'

Not only princes, of course, are subject to contumely. On this day in 1838, Nathaniel Hawthorne recorded in his diary having fallen into conversation with a 'pedlar' or travelling salesman, who sold essences of aniseed and cloves, hair-oil, cologne, and the like. 'He spoke of the trials of temper to which pedlars are subjected, but said that it was necessary to be forbearing, because the same road must be travelled again and again. The pedlars find satisfaction for all *contumelies* in making good bargains out of their customers.' An admirable attitude.

28 July

Sciomachy

You might not often need a word for 'battle with a shadow', but when you do you'll be glad that there's *sciomachy*. The shadows, of course, are usually metaphorical, so that *sciomachy* is something like pointless shadow-boxing. Dr Johnson cites an essay by Abraham Cowley, relating a 'vision' or dream he had about Oliver Cromwell: 'To avoid this *sciomachy*, or imaginary combat of words, let me know, sir, what you mean by the name of tyrant?'

The royalist Cowley, a poet and playwright, was much admired by his peers: having died on this day in 1667, he was buried in Westminster Abbey alongside Chaucer and Spenser. He features in Samuel Johnson's *Lives of the Poets*, but his posthumous reputation had otherwise declined rapidly, prompting Alexander Pope to ask, in 1737, 'Who now reads Cowley?' Well, we just did.

Petrichor

Today is Rain Day, because in the town of Waynesburg, Philadelphia, it rains on 29 July remarkably often. Let us then welcome the summer downpour with the beautiful word *petrichor*, which means 'the smell of the earth after rain at the end of a dry spell'. *Petro–* means 'having to do with rock' (hence *petroleum*, Latin for 'rock oil'), and *ichor* is the mythical fluid that supposedly flowed in the veins of the Greek gods, and so in geology the name for a fluid or emanation from magma.

The term was coined in 1964 by the Australian geochemists Isabel Joy Bear and Richard G. Thomas, in their paper about the organic components of the smell, called 'Nature of Argillaceous Odour'. *Argillaceous* ('like clay') was what this scent had previously been termed, but the authors pointed out that its appearance was not limited to clay-based soils. So they named it to describe that '"tenuous essence" derived from rock or stone'. Happy *petrichor* season.

Wuthering

Made famous first by Emily Brontë (born on this day in 1818) and then again by Kate Bush (born on the same date 140 years later), *wuthering* might sound like a made-up term of doominess, perhaps a darker form of *withering*. In fact, as aficionados of the blasted heath know, it is an old weather-word for 'characterized by strong winds', as well as, more generally, a 'rushing, whizzing, blustering' (*OED*). *Wuthering* is an alternate spelling of *whithering*, which via the Old English *hwiþa* derives from the Old Norse for 'squall'.

It can also mean a great noise, as in Julia Strachey's 1951 novel *The Man on the Pier*, where she writes of the 'routine hours that are without inspiration in a day – those spent in buying stamps for letters, in filing receipts, in the dreary wuthering of machineries, in the changings from place to place'. Few others seem to have dared to employ the word since *Wuthering Heights* made it Brontë's own in 1847, but it is surely too beautiful not to slip into one's next conversation about the unseasonal weather.

31 July

Panurgic

In those moments when you feel ready and able to do anything at all, you are experiencing the thrilling sensation of being *panurgic*. The Greek *pan* ('all') and *ergos* ('work') combine to form a word that, when applied to others, can mean either admirably multi-skilled, or unnecessarily meddling. The great French novelist Rabelais named one of his characters Panurge: he is a multilingual knave who famously gets his revenge on a sheep merchant he thinks has overcharged him for one of the beasts by throwing it over the side of their boat. The rest of the herd, sheeplike, all follow their leader into the sea and drown.

On the other hand, *panurgic* can be meant as sincere praise, as one nineteenth-century writer spoke of Denis Diderot – who died on this day in 1784 – as a '*panurgic* and ... encyclopaedic critic'; or as an ironical admixture of praise and criticism, as the Irish writer John Francis Byrne referred in his memoirs to a former prime minister as 'Lloyd George the Panurgic'. Perhaps the urge to be *panurgic* is one that, after all, should be interrogated.

AUGUST

1 August

Tenty

The Scottish poet Sir Richard Maitland, who is thought by some to have died on this day in 1586, is the first writer recorded as having used the word *tenty*, which does not mean 'like a tent', but 'watchful' and 'cautious'. It derives from the Old French *tentif*, short for *ententif*, as does the synonym *attentive*, but *tenty* arguably has a more active, energetic feel.

In 1555, Maitland wrote a poem addressed to his eldest son William, who had gone into politics and been appointed secretary to Mary, Queen of Scots. 'Be wise, and *tentie*, in thy governing,' Richard advised his son; 'and try them well in whom thou wilt confide [be careful who you confide in].' No doubt his son tried to follow this advice, but as someone in another world once said, when you play the game of thrones, you win or you die. And even the most *tenty* fellow could still end up dying, as William Maitland did, in prison.

Nithing

A particularly egregious coward or villain may be called a *nithing*, a word of deep antiquity that comes from an old Icelandic root for 'enmity'. The historian Edward Augustus Freeman, born on this day in 1823, explains the bargain struck with his people by King Rufus, son of William the Conqueror, with two proclamations. According to the first, 'The days of King Eadward were to come back; all wrong was to be undone; no more unrighteous taxes were to be raised; each man was again, as in the days of Cnut, to have his free right of hunting on his own land.' In exchange, however, the second proclamation announced that 'the shameful name of *nithing* was to be the doom of every man, French or English, who failed to obey the summons of his lord the King.'

Nithing can also be used adjectivally to mean 'utterly without honour' or 'wholly contemptible'. It has nothing to do with *nothing*, but perhaps the half-rhyme still lends the insult a particular force to modern ears.

Bibacity

The doctor Thomas Trotter was baptized on this day in 1760, and after a career as Physician to the Fleet, published the first book-length inquiry into what we now call alcoholism, entitled *An Essay, Medical, Philosophical, and Chemical, on Drunkenness, and its Effects on the Human Body* (1804). He was perhaps the first to suggest that 'the habit of drunkenness is a disease of the mind', while enumerating 'the evils which follow *bibacity*'. From the Latin *bibere* ('to drink'), *bibacity* has been used to span the spectrum from a regular fondness for merriment to awful dependence. Dr Johnson defines *bibacious* as 'much addicted to drinking', while Henry Cockeram's 1623 dictionary says *bibacity* is 'outrageous drinking'.

The least moralistic of our lexicographers is good old Thomas Blount, who defines *bibacity* as 'great or courageous drinking or quaffing', but those were, perhaps, more innocent times.

4 AUGUST

Esculent

Food-lovers are always in search of fancy new ways to describe food, so they could do worse than revive the term *esculent*, meaning 'anything that you can eat'. In 1626, Francis Bacon warned, 'A Number of Herbs are not *Esculent* at all', while in 1633 we find mentioned: 'A piece of Suffolk cheese, or Gammon of Bacon, Or any *esculent*, as the learned call it.' (The word comes from the Latin *esca*, 'food', whereas *succulent* comes from *succus*, meaning 'juice'.)

It was once the custom, on this day, for British people to make grottoes out of oyster shells, in order to celebrate the end of the 'closed' season for oyster beds. So, it was explained in 1863, 'the 4th of August was the period when the juicy *esculent* could first be enjoyed, after a long interval of reticence'. *Bon appétit.*

Aerumnous

If the world is weighing on your shoulders, you may sigh that it is an *aerumnous* place, this being an evocative term for 'full of troubles'. The word first appears in a 1658 dictionary entitled *The New World of English Words* by Edward Phillips, who was born around this time in 1630. Phillips was a nephew of John Milton, and was taught by him; later, for a time, he worked as the great poet's assistant. His dictionary, though, was attacked for being mainly plagiarized from Thomas Blount's earlier *Glossographia*. At least, though, *aerumnus* doesn't feature in the latter dictionary, so we can sincerely thank Phillips for finding it, or perhaps even coining it himself from the Latin (*aerumna*, 'affliction' or 'distress').

In his later years, we learn, Phillips was a poor schoolmaster in the Strand, and 'wrote and translated several things merely to get a bare livelihood', his own life being no less *aerumnous* than our own.

Abaddon

Ambrose Bierce, in *The Devil's Dictionary*, offers this mysterious definition: 'ABBADON, *n*. A certain person who is much in society, but whom one does not meet. A bad one.' In so describing *Abaddon*, Bierce is evoking the very devil himself, for that is one of his names. In the King James Bible, it is written: 'And they had a king over them, which is the angel of the bottomless pit, whose name in the Hebrew tongue is *Abaddon*.'

Alfred Tennyson, born on this day in 1809, has his hero in 'St Simeon Stylites' describe what life was like before he ascended his pillar: 'On the coals I lay, / A vessel full of sin: all hell beneath / Made me boil over. Devils pluck'd my sleeve; / *Abaddon* and Asmodeus [another prince of hell] caught at me.' The name *Abaddon* retains a bleak, lonely grandeur, used metaphorically or otherwise. And remember Bierce's warning: you can meet him without knowing it.

Roxy

On this day in 1971, *Melody Maker* carried the first big article about an upcoming band called Roxy Music. Singer Bryan Ferry has said that the name of the band was meant to recall a vanished age of plush theatres and dancehalls, since many such establishments were called The Roxy. But why?

The first Roxy Theatre, a 6,000-seat movie palace that cost eight million dollars to build, was opened in New York City in 1927, and was so called because Roxy was the nickname of the manager, film mogul Samuel Lionel Rothafel. In showbusiness, the term *Roxy ending* means a big fanfare at the end of a number, since that's how they did it at the original theatre. In English, *roxy* is also a rather sublime adjective meaning 'over-ripe' or 'nearly rotten': one can apply it to fruit, but perhaps also to an atmosphere of distressed velvet and seedy glamour.

Clowder

Today being International Cat Day, let us celebrate the eternal feline by reclaiming the earliest recorded collective noun for a group of cats, which is *clowder*, from 1801. Other terms have been used: you could also say a *glaring* of cats, though that seems likely to have been coined by an ailurophobe (one with an irrational fear of cats), as too must have been the highly prejudicial phrase a *destruction* of cats. A *pounce* of cats, on the other hand, is quite picturesque, capturing the athletic spring ever present even in the animals' regal stillness.

Clowder, meanwhile, derives from the old dialect noun *clodder*, meaning 'a clotted or curdled mass, a clot', and the verb *cludder*, 'to crowd, heap, or cluster together', from where we also get *clutter*. A *clowder* of cats, then, seems quite appropriate to the animals' aristocratic anarchism, their disdain for order and rules – or, at least, for those designed by mere humans.

Twitterpated

This day in 1942 saw the release of Disney's film *Bambi*, which gifted to the world a new word for 'besotted'. 'Ev'rything is *twitterpated* in the Spring,' runs one song lyric, because all the animals and plants are in love. The term *twitterpated*, coined (or at least popularized) by one of the credited songwriters – Helen Bliss, Robert Sour, or Henry Manners – is a combination of *twitter* (meaning 'excitement', as in *all a-twitter*) and *pated* (meaning 'headed'), creating a pleasant sense of light-headed thrill.

Twitterpated was adopted straight away by eager writers to mean 'smitten' or 'excited', and then saw a slightly sad shift in meaning towards 'foolish', 'scatter-brained', or 'bird-witted', as it was glossed in 1959. (A reviewer of *A Series of Unfortunate Events* in 2004 described Meryl Streep's character as 'a well-meaning but *twitterpated* guardian'.) To revive it now in its original joyous sense of 'lovestruck' might seem an uphill battle, but it would be good to reclaim a *twitter* as something positive.

10 AUGUST

Araneous

On this day in 1962, the comic *Amazing Fantasy* printed the first ever appearance of Spider-Man, in honour of whom let us resurrect the word *araneous*. It first appears in the eccentrically evocative definition by Thomas Blount in his *Glossographia*: '*Araneous*, full of spiders' webs.' The word is derived from the same Greek root (*arachne*: 'spider') as *arachnoid*, but there is something more mazy and weblike to the sound of *araneous*, and so it was adopted in medicine and botany to describe various kinds of filmy substance, such as 'the *araneous* filaments' of a plant's leaves (1693), or 'the curious *Araneous* Membrane' of the eye (1713). Spider-Man, of course, entraps his enemies by wrapping them up in the powerful strands of his *araneous* web-fluid.

11 August

Obreption

Who is that sneaking up behind you? It is someone practised in the art of *obreption*, from the Latin *obreptio* ('to creep up unseen'). This creepy term has been applied to unwanted thoughts as well as unwanted people, and also has a more general sense of 'fraud' or 'impropriety'. The seventeenth-century English lexicographer Randle Cotgrave defined *obreption* thus: 'the creeping, or stealing to a thing by crafty means'.

A nice distinction exists between *obreption*, fraudulently obtaining something – an ecclesiastical dispensation, or royal gifts – by means of stating a falsehood, and *subreption*, fraudulently obtaining something by suppressing the truth. Many people, of course, are guilty of both at the same time, such as Charles Ponzi, adept at the type of kleptocratic fraud that became known as a 'Ponzi scheme': his own fell apart on this day in 1920, when the Boston bank he controlled was seized, and he was arrested the next morning. As long as such cheating and swindling remain with us, the particularly stern charge of *obreption* should have its use.

12 August

Sesquipedalian

In his *Ars Poetica*, the Roman poet Horace counselled young poets against using *sesquipedalia verba* – 'foot-and-a-half-long words'. And so *sesquipedalian* was adopted into English for needlessly polysyllabic writing. The Romantic poet Robert Southey, born on this day in 1774, was much abused by Byron, but was not above abusing other poets himself, writing of one previous practitioner: 'The verses of Stephen Hawes are as full of barbarous *sesquipedalian* Latinisms.'

As a noun, *sesquipedalian* can also mean a *sesquipedalian* word, creating a vertigo-inducing regress. So it was used by the anonymous reviewer of the religious poetry of one William Phillips, in *Fraser's Magazine* of April 1830, which is a hatchet job of thrillingly unrelenting rudeness. The writer quotes Milton and then announces: 'We have here described a true poem, written by a true poet. We now beg to turn the attention of our readers to the gesticulations of an ape.' He goes on: 'How any individual, who has received the rudiments of the commonest polite education, could have sat down to waste his time in writing such utter and contemptible trash is to us most astonishing … what an amazing power in writing down hard names and *sesquipedalians*.' Truly, they do not write like this any more.

Ambisinistrous

This being International Lefthanders Day, it is past time for us *cuddy-wifters* to reclaim the sinister insult *ambisinistrous*, which literally means 'having two left hands' and so, according to ancient bigotry, 'clumsy'. (It is the opposite of *ambidextrous*, which means having two right hands.) In honour of fellow left-handers such as Jimi Hendrix and John McEnroe, we should rather use *ambisinistrous* to mean 'uncommonly skilled with the hands'.

The term also appears in a rather salacious sense in the gossipy reminiscences of the nineteenth-century army officer and writer William Pitt Lennox, who writes thus of the Prince of Wales, later King George IV: 'The Prince did not content himself with his left-handed bride. In wedlock, if he can[not] be said to have been ambidextrous, he was certainly more than *ambisinistrous*. In short, the sinister handlings of his Royal Highness are not easily to be computed.'

14 August

Recrudescence

The novelist John Galsworthy was born on this day in 1867. In his novel of postwar decadence, *To Let* (1921) – a volume in what was later called The Forsyte Saga – the hero, Soames, learns in the newspaper that a cousin he never liked, Jolyon, has died. 'That quick-blooded sentiment hatred had run its course long since in Soames's heart, and he had refused to allow any *recrudescence*, but he considered this early decease a piece of poetic justice.'

Recrudescence comes from the Latin for 'to become raw again', and since 1665 it has usually, as above, been applied to the recurrence of something undesirable, particularly medical symptoms or disease. Confusingly, however, it has also been used to mean the reappearance of something good, or even a kind of spiritual resurrection, as an artist might be said to experience a *recrudescence* of creative passion. The *OED* cites, as an example of this positive sense, a nineteenth-century critic observing that 'There has been of late a *recrudescence* of Wordsworthianism,' but one is at liberty to imagine that the sly writer meant it as cause for alarm.

15 AUGUST

Pandiculation

Perhaps the pleasantest thing to do upon waking up, like a cat, is to have a good stretch, an activity that the term *pandiculation* makes sound even more agreeable. It derives straightforwardly from the Latin *pandere*, 'to stretch', and was employed from 1611 in medical writing. Later, it was also used to mean 'yawning', perhaps because the two so often go together.

More picturesquely, the word is employed virtuosically as metaphor by Thomas De Quincey, born on this day in 1785. In the preface to his *Confessions of an English Opium-Eater* (1821), De Quincey begs the reader to accept everything he writes as though he had proven it, or else he will be forced in subsequent revisions to expand – or *pandiculate* – the book with tremendously dull detail. 'No, believe all that I ask of you,' he writes, 'for if not, then in the next edition of my Opium Confessions, revised and enlarged, I will make you believe and tremble; and *à force d'ennuyer* [simply by being so boring], by mere dint of *pandiculation* I will terrify readers of mine from ever again questioning any postulate that I shall think fit to make.' A splendid threat.

Adlubescence

To emphasize how nice something is, you might say it brings *adlubescence*, a charming word meaning 'pleasure' or 'delight'. Dr Johnson gives it in an even more obscure form, as *allubescency*, but *adlubescence* makes clearer the derivation: Latin *ad*, 'to', plus *lubet* (or *libet*), 'it pleases'. The poet Andrew Marvell, who died on this day in 1678, uses it in a 1673 pamphlet attacking the clergyman Samuel Parker, who had given approval for a book slandering Baptists in New England to be published. 'I dare undertake,' Marvell writes sarcastically, 'that when he came to the Licensing of that Pamphlet, he felt such an expansion of heart, such an *adlubescence* of mind, and such an exaltation of spirit, that betwixt Joy and Love he could scarce refrain from kissing it.'

As it happens, the root of *adlubescence*, Latin *ad libet*, is also where we get *ad lib*, which was originally a marking in musical scores indicating that the instrument needn't play exactly what was written down, and so came to mean any kind of improvisation. So a good *ad lib* from a saxophonist or comedian could bring the audience *adlubescence*.

17 August

Emacity

One might today choose to signal resistance to unthinking consumerism by making a more ecologically minded second-hand purchase in honour of Thrift Shop Day, and so to perform a slightly more virtuous form of *emacity*. This is one of those archaic terms that seems more relevant than ever to the modern age, since it means, according to Thomas Blount in 1656, 'a desire to be always buying'. From the Latin *emere*, 'to buy', the word came into its own in the nineteenth century, along with the invention of shopping as recreation.

So, writers of the age thought, emacity was a 'disease' or 'itch for buying bargains'. (One attributed the word to Sir Thomas Urquhart, the Scottish writer who described himself as a 'logofascinated spirit', unquenchably interested in words, and so might well have been the uncredited coiner.) Compared with its modern equivalents – the facetious *shopaholism* and the contradictory *retail therapy* – *emacity*, with its whisper of infection and moral malnutrition, warrants revival.

Rhadamanthine

In Greek mythology, Rhadamanthus was a son of Zeus and Europa. While alive he was a king of Crete known for the unwavering justice of his rule (some sources suggested he passed a law allowing for self-defence), and afterwards he was made a judge in the Underworld. And so, what is *rhadamanthine* is strict and unswerving in its judgement.

Watching a murder trial in Paris in 1839, Thackeray thought there was far too little evidence for conviction: he wrote to a friend that the 'romantic' prosecutor chose 'to compose and recite a little drama, and draw tears from juries', but hoped that 'severe *Rhadamanthine* judges are not to be melted by such trumpery'. The accused, Sébastian Peytel, was nonetheless found guilty of killing his wife, and later guillotined. Even the public intervention of the novelist Honoré de Balzac – who died on this day in 1850 – could not save Peytel from a fate so *rhadamanthine*.

Pervicacious

A person who is *pervicacious* is extremely obstinate, or as Dr Johnson puts it: 'Spitefully obstinate; peevishly contumacious [insubordinate].' Lest you think here of *perverted*, that is a false cousin: 'pervert' comes from the Latin *pervertere*, 'to turn around' or 'turn the wrong way', while *pervicacious* is derived from *pervincere*, 'to prevail' or 'win over'. In English, though, a *pervicacious* person is not merely one who prevails, but one who is determined to do so at all costs: someone thoroughly headstrong.

In *Clarissa* by Samuel Richardson — baptized on this day in 1689 — the heroine's brother James tells her that she is 'one of the most *pervicacious* young creatures that ever was heard of!' Other phenomena deemed *pervicacious* are donkeys wandering into a field of barley, and theatrical audiences who, as it was written in 1973, are 'a *pervicacious* horde of floating voters, [who] rush confidently to support the worst candidate on offer'. Not, then, unlike actual voters.

Conquassate

On this day in 1866, Andrew Johnson issued a presidential proclamation declaring that the American Civil War was officially over. One of the soldiers who fought in that war, George Norton Galloway, published an account of his Pennsylvania regiment's activities, in which we find this wry poem dedicated to the pine trees with which his men built huts: 'Oh! Vegetable coniferous! / Conoid and conoidical! / Consanguineous of the "Balm of Gilead", / Conjunctively sylvanus, / We *conquassate*, or "Yank" thy branches, / And in consarcination [patching together] we confiscate thee for our ranches.'

To *conquassate* indeed means 'to yank', or otherwise to pull or shake violently, from the Latin *quatere*, to shake – whether trees or other inanimate objects, or parts of one's own person. ('Vomits do violently *conquassate* the Lungs,' warned a doctor in 1666.) Sometimes *shake* or *agitate* are not strong enough, and only the evocative *conquassate* will do.

Bahuvrihi

In grammar, a *bahuvrihi* is a compound phrase (usually an adjective plus a noun) that is used as a possessive adjective to describe some quality of another noun, e.g. 'rosy-fingered dawn', 'high-potency vitamins', 'a bushy-tailed cat', and so forth. Lady Mary Wortley Montagu, who died on this day in 1762, writes in 'A Receipt to Cure the Vapours': 'Why will Delia thus retire, / And idly languish life away? / While the sighing crowd admire, / 'Tis too soon for hartshorn tea.' *Hartshorn tea* here is a *bahuvrihi*, describing a medicinal infusion literally made from the horns of the male red deer. Sometimes the *bahuvrihi* is used on its own as the name for the thing with the characteristics it describes, as with 'waxwing', a bird with red wingtips that were thought to resemble sealing-wax.

The word *bahuvrihi* was adopted for this form in the nineteenth century directly from the Sanskrit for 'having much rice', which in turns comes from *bahú* (much) and *vrīhí* (rice). Happily, then, *bahuvrihi* is itself a *bahuvrihi*.

Facinorous

Richard III died on this day in 1485, and passed into history and literature as one of England's most villainous kings – especially for having, it is assumed, ordered the murders of the Princes in the Tower. In a 1548 chronicle of his reign, it is called that '*facinorous* act'. The word *facinorous* (from the Latin for 'criminal') is reserved for the most vile, wicked, or heinous behaviour imaginable.

In George Walker's 1799 novel *The Vagabond*, meanwhile, the character Frederick, a satirical portrait of contemporary philosophers, asks: 'When shall the *ingannations* [see 19 October] of prejudice be delacerated, and the *catachrestical* [see 9 November] reasonings of *facinorous* aristocrats be disbanded by the *zetetic* [see 16 February] spirit of the eighteenth century?' We are, perhaps, still waiting.

Remord

On this day in 1637, riots broke out in Edinburgh upon the first use of the Book of Common Prayer in Scotland. The edition contained translations of the Psalms by William Alexander, poet and 1st Earl of Stirling, who in his epic poem describing the end of the world, aptly entitled *Doomes-day* (1614), writes: 'When troubled conscience reads accusing scrolls, / Which witnessed are even by the breast's own brood; / O what a terrour wounds *remording* soules, / Who poison find what seem'd a pleasant food!'

To recall something with regret or remorse is to *remord*, from the Latin *remordere*, 'to bite again'. One may *remord* intransitively, as Stirling's souls do, or one may *remord* a specific action or choice made in the past. This being a universal human affliction, it may help, instead of having to say 'to remember with regret', to revive the plain strong word *remord*.

24 August

Wayzgoose

Today is St Bartholemew's Day, and marks the point at which printers in the seventeenth century would henceforth need to work for part of the day by candlelight. To celebrate the occasion, the master printer would take his workforce out for a big party, consisting of a well-lubricated feast and some-times also an outing into the country. This event was called the *wayzgoose* (or *waygoose*). As the mathematical printer and lexicographer Joseph Moxon explained in 1683: 'These *Way-gooses*, are always kept about Bartholomew-tide. And till the Master-Printer have given this *Way-goose*, the Journey-men do not use to Work by Candle Light.'

Why *waygoose*, or *wayzgoose*? No one is sure. Perhaps goose was the main course at the feast; if so, perhaps (as Nathan Bailey's 1730 dictionary, *Dictionarium Britannicum*, suggests) it is another term for 'stubble-goose', a traditional autumn dish. In any case the *wayzgoose* has, perhaps sur-prisingly, survived into the present millennium, as in 2005 a Cheshire newspaper reported a local printing firm having its '*wayzgoose* (traditional printers' outing)' at a local Italian restaurant.

Onolatry

If you know someone who worships donkeys, you may accuse him of *onolatry*, from the Greek *onos*, 'ass', and *–latry*, 'excessive worship' (as in *idolatry*). Very interesting, you say, but who has cause to use it? The mocking charge of *onolatry* was originally made by the ancient Romans against Jews (who were supposed to worship a donkey-god) and then Christians: the famous Alexamenos graffito shows an early Christian worshipping a crucified man with a donkey's head.

Such religious slanders might by now be outdated, but *onolatry* is also more widely useful to describe excessive devotion to something foolish. So an admiring writer said in 1924 that Friedrich Nietzsche – who died on this day in 1900 – had 'depicted the leaders of the nineteenth century as engaged in a veritable *onolatry* or ass-worship'. It would surely strain credulity to suppose that there were no *onolatries* current today.

Tsundoku

There is no English equivalent of this Japanese term, even though the practice is ubiquitous: *tsundoku* means not reading a book after you have bought it, but simply adding it to the pile of your other unread books. It originated in the nineteenth century as a slang combination of the Japanese terms for 'piling things up' and 'books'. The writer and publisher Alfred Edward Newton, who was born on this day in 1863, had a surprise hit with his book *The Amenities of Book-Collecting and Kindred Affections* (1918), and wrote elsewhere: 'It is my pleasure to buy more books than I can read. Who was it who said, "I hold the buying of more books than one can peradventure read, as nothing less than the soul's reaching towards infinity; which is the only thing that raises us above the beasts that perish"?'

So remember that acquiring books is a noble end in itself, even if you don't read them; rest assured that the authors still get their royalty.

Sequacious

One who is *sequacious* is an unquestioning acolyte, a slavish adherent of some person or school of thought, and probably a practitioner of *psittacism* (see 14 November) to boot. It is derived from the Latin *sequax*, 'a follower', and can also be used of biddable beasts, or tractable objects, though its psychological meaning seems still the most relevant. The poet and playwright James Thomson, who died on this day in 1748, defined a philosopher as one opposed to the *sequacious* multitude in his poem *Summer*, part of *The Four Seasons* (1730): 'The vulgar stare; amazement is their joy, / And mystic faith, a fond *sequacious* herd! / But scrutinous *Philosophy* looks deep, / With piercing eye, into the latent cause; / Nor can she swallow what she does not see.'

The identification of any modern collection of persons that might be thought to comprise a *sequacious herd* is left as an exercise to the reader.

28 AUGUST

Felicificability

What is *felicific* is productive of happiness, and so the opposite of *malefic* (see 14 September). The word is particularly associated with the nineteenth-century utilitarian philosophers. Henry Sidgwick, who died on this day in 1900, writes in his *The Methods of Ethics*: 'It will be convenient to use the terms "felicific" and "infelicific" for "productive of happiness and the reverse".'

Happily, though, what is *felicificative*, or 'happy-making', is not restricted to such technical discourse, and one's *felicificability*, or 'capacity for happiness' (coined by the philosopher John Grote in 1865) may always be filled by learning new words for what is *felicious*, or happy.

Slubberdegullion

The past is full of beautiful insults that might enrich modern spats, one of which is *slubberdegullion*, for a slovenly or filthy person. To *slubber* means to make dirty, perhaps from the Dutch for 'wading through mud', and a *gullion* is a wretch or soak. In Samuel Butler's mock-heroic romp *Hudibras* (1684), the Amazon warrior Trulla beats up the eponymous knight, and then shows a contemptuous mercy: 'Although thou hast deserv'd, / Base *slubberdegullion*, to be serv'd / As thou didst vow to deal with me, / If thou hadst got the victory; / Yet I shall rather act a part / That suits my fame than thy desert.'

Meanwhile, in the Jacobean play *The Custom of the Country*, a young woman has just been married, and the disgusting local Count is demanding his *droit de seigneur*, or the ancient right to have sex with the new bride. 'Must this *slubberdegullion* / Have her maiden-head now?' asks the groom's distressed brother. Spoiler: he does not. The play was written by Philip Massinger and the great John Fletcher, who died of the plague on this day in 1625.

Pareidolia

This word was imported into English from the German (*Pareidolien*) by the translators of the Swiss psychiatrist Karl Jaspers's *General Psychopathology* in 1962, and describes seeing patterns or images in random visual stimuli. (As a later text-book described it, '*Pareidolia* is seeing images in a poorly structured visual field, e.g. in old walls, clouds, wallpaper, carpets.') Of course, we all do this from time to time, and Hamlet teases Polonius by getting him to agree that a cloud looks first like one animal, then another. ('Very like a whale,' the old man amicably agrees.) On this day in 1976, the orbiter Viking 1 took the second of two photographs of the surface of Mars featuring a rock formation that looked eerily human and became known as the 'Face on Mars'. (Later missions taking higher-resolution images, disappointingly, proved this had been merely a trick of the light.)

Even computers are prone to *pareidolia*: machine-learning systems trained on image analysis can themselves be induced to hallucinate absent forms. Metaphorically, you might even say that *pareidolia*, in the sense of the mental habit of trying to impose order upon a chaotic world, is simply the human condition.

Gobemouche

This splendid insult is formed from the French *gober* (to swallow or gulp) plus *mouches* (flies). A fly-swallower is one whose mouth is constantly open in amazement, and so a credulous or gullible person. One writer for the *Pall Mall Gazette* in 1884 fulminated against 'Those Continental *gobemouches* whose gift for believing the incredible almost approaches to genius', which is rather ungrateful, given that he acquired the word from the continent in the first place. Balance is restored by the travel writer Richard Ford, who died on this day in 1858. In his *A Hand-Book for Travellers in Spain* (1845), he warned English tourists against believing the tall tales told by the locals, whose 'idle stories are often believed by the *gobemouche* class of book-making travellers'.

The passage of time does not seem to have reduced the numbers of the *gobemouche* classes.

September

1 September

Exiguous

What is *exiguous* (Latin *exiguus*) is tiny in size or number, meagre, or of little consequence. Fittingly, its first appearance in English is as an example of rhetorical *litotes* (see 3 December), with the author of the eulogy *Eliah's Wish* (1630), Robert Willian, dedicating his '*exiguous* tract' to his patron, and widow of the sermon's subject, the Viscountess of Sudbury. Similarly, the poet Siegfried Sasson, who died on this day in 1967, refers in his memoir to the war journal he kept as 'my *exiguous* diary'.

Exiguous, happily, could also be used in mock-heroic style, as the early eighteenth-century poet John Philips refers grandly to mice as 'the race *exiguous*, uninur'd to wet', and by various people down the centuries who complained of low pay or trifling points made by their opponents, both of which *exiguous* phenomena, alas, are still with us.

Feculent

If you are groping for a word strong enough to express just how disgusting something is, the word *feculent* awaits. It shares its Latin root with *faeces*, but has been liberally applied since the fifteenth century to whatever writers have considered most noxious, from garbage or polluted rivers, to the plebeians, and even all 'the most *feculent* corruptions of modern civilization'.

The English philanthropist John Howard, born on this day in 1726, was inspired by his spell of involuntary residence in a French dungeon to become a pioneering penal reformer. Among the aspects of contemporary prisons he inveighed against was improper ventilation, for, as he wrote in 1780, 'Air which has performed its office in the lungs, is *feculent* and noxious.' The example of another eighteenth-century scribe, who wrote of a rival's work that 'Every Word here is *feculent* and stinks,' shows that the word will also do fine work as a literary insult.

Imbrue

To stain something is to *imbrue* it – with meat-juice, hot pitch, berries, or – as it might be, and too often was – with blood. It comes from the Old French *embreuver,* to soak (often in liquor), which in turn derives at last from the Latin *bibere*, to drink.

Oliver Cromwell, who died on this day in 1658, had used the word in a letter written on this day in 1649, describing the enemy he had just defeated at the siege of Drogheda, in Ireland, as 'These barbarous wretches, who have *imbrued* their hands in so much innocent blood', which was argu-ably a bit rich coming from someone whose forces had just massacred priests and friars, as well as the defending soldiers, and burned others alive in a church. For the Irish, this action *imbrued* Cromwell's memory for ever more.

4 September

Nefandous

What is *nefandous*, the Latin root informs us, is simply not to be spoken of. Of course, by calling something *nefandous*, you are speaking of it, so the word is really used for whatever the author wishes to suggest is absolutely abominable: crimes, blasphemies, and whatnot. In an 1862 article for the *Atlantic*, Oliver Wendell Holmes, Sr., recalls meeting an army surgeon trained in Edinburgh: 'He had been brought very close to that immane [monstrous] and *nefandous* Burke-and-Hare business which made the blood of civilization run cold in the year 1828, and told me, in a very calm way, with an occasional pinch from the mull, to refresh his memory, some of the details of those frightful murders, never rivalled in horror …' Our army surgeon certainly couldn't help speaking of what is unspeakable.

William Burke and William Hare were the men who murdered sixteen people between 1827 and 1828 and sold their bodies to the anatomist Robert Knox, who used them in his lectures. To be fair to Knox, who was born on this day in 1791 and was subsequently vilified for his involvement (Walter Scott called him a 'learned carcass-butcher'), most authorities agree that he did not know these handy cadavers had been expressly killed for the purpose.

Scaramouch

The singer Freddie Mercury, who was born on this day in 1946, wonders in 'Bohemian Rhapsody' whether *Scaramouch* will do the fandango. It is certainly possible that he will: the fandango is a Spanish dance, and *Scaramouch*, while Italian in origin, was usually portrayed as a Spanish character. Originally *Scaramuccia* (literally, 'skirmisher'), he was a stock figure in Italian farce, a scampish boaster, much beaten about by Harlequin. Thanks to a successful visit of Italian players to London in 1673, there was a craze for references to the figure by poets and writers including Andrew Marvell and Thomas Shadwell, who in his comedy *The Virtuoso* has the orator Sir Formal Trifle enter dressed 'in Scaramoucha's habit'.

Later, a *scaramouch* was any kind of rascally person. In George Meredith's novel *Rhoda Fleming* (1865), the aged porter Anthony confesses: 'Once I was an idle young *scaramouch.*' Weren't we all?

Ubiety

If you wish to speak of the 'whereness' of some thing or person, you have at your disposal the more refined word *ubiety*. From the Latin *ubi* ('where'), it can be used simply to mean *location*, but also something more like 'the necessity of being somewhere': as, for instance, in the philosopher C. J. Ducasse's contention in *Nature, Mind, and Death* (1951) that 'Physical existence, thus, is essentially spatiotemporal *ubiety*; and that which has or lacks *ubiety*, that is, is or is not present at some place in space at some time, is always some what or kind – which may be a kind of substance, or of property, or of relation, or of activity, or of change, or of state, and so on.'

Fair enough, you say; but *ubiety* can also conjure an even more metaphysical sense of placeness. Or so you might think when stoned, as the English poet Philip James Bailey – who died on this day in 1902 – almost certainly was before or during the composition of his poem 'A Spiritual Legend', in which he expatiates upon 'Vervain [a medicinal plant] and magic haschisch, which endows / Thought with *ubiety*, and waking mind / Clothes with the dread delight of dreams; and kiff, / Soul gifting with expansive extasie.'

Neoteric

If something is particularly zeitgeisty and modern in outlook, you could call it *neoteric*, from the Greek *neoteros*, 'newer'. It was once commonly used as the opposite of *ancient* or *antique*, and then came to be applied to contemporaries with new ideas: '*neoteric* authors' (1822) and '*neoteric* Sages' (1876). This was not always meant admiringly; indeed, *neoteric* can also be used with scepticism, to mean novel but shallow, or 'newfangled': writers spoke of '*neoteric* jargon' (1816), or, marvellously, 'the *neoteric* fashion of spending a honeymoon on the railway' (1879).

The poet Edith Sitwell, who was born on this day in 1887, employed *neoteric* positively, to mean 'bringing forth what is new', in her poem 'Anne Boleyn's Song': 'In the *neoteric* Spring the winter coldness / Will be forgotten / As I forget the coldness of my last lover ...'

Pataphysics

The French writer and absurdist playwright Alfred Jarry, author of *Ubu Roi*, was born on this day in 1873. One of his gifts to the world was the absurdist discipline, or perhaps anti-discipline, of *pataphysics*: notionally, the study of anything that eludes precise scientific or other description. Jarry coined the word (in French, *pataphysique*) in 1907, explaining that it was short for *epimetaphysics*. (Aristotle's *metaphysics* was all the stuff that went 'beyond physics', so *epimetataphysics* was all the stuff that went beyond that.) An ironic and playful formulation, certainly, describing the absurdist irony of his art, but by no means simply facetious. To this day there are pataphysical societies in London, New York City, Portland, and elsewhere. *Pataphysics*, Jarry explained, was 'the science of imaginary solutions, an exact science and a liberal art'. When real solutions fail us, why not try imaginary ones?

Ennead

On the ninth day of the ninth month, let us celebrate the word *ennead*, which means 'a group of nine things'. It comes down to us from the Phoenician-born philosopher Porphyry, active in the third century CE, who studied with the neo-Platonist Plotinus and edited his teacher's works, calling them the *Enneads*: six volumes, each containing nine books. This is neat because 6 is a perfect number (it is the sum of its divisors: 1 + 2 + 3), while 9 is a square number (3 × 3), and there were also nine Muses. To make such a numerologically neat division, as it turns out, Porphyry artificially divided some of Plotinus's books into more than one part, but that we can surely forgive.

Later on, some classical composers shared a superstition that you would die after completing an *ennead* of symphonies: Beethoven's, Bruckner's, and Mahler's 9ths were all their last. This perhaps bespeaks some eldritch connection between music and cats, who enjoy an *ennead* of lives and no more.

10 September

Snollygoster

In 1952, Harry Truman rebuked politicians who prayed in public in order to seem pious and virtuous. 'I wish some of these *snollygosters* would read the New Testament and perform accordingly,' he said. Some of these what? Truman later glossed *snollygoster*, perhaps winkingly, as 'a man born out of wedlock', but it is in fact a nineteenth-century term for an unscrupulous, ambitious politician.

The American journalist William Safire did much to give the word new currency after Truman had brought it back, and it was enthusiastically adopted by, among others, the TV host and culture warrior Bill O'Reilly, who was born on this day in 1949. But where does it come from? Perhaps the German *schnelle Geister*, literally 'quick spirits' or 'quick ghosts', but also used to denote the 'Wild Host', which in old Germanic myth is a supernatural hunting party that terrorizes the forest at night. This phrase, it is supposed, could have given rise to the name of a mythical Maryland beast called the *snallygaster*, which was half bird of prey and half reptile, and was said 'to prey on poultry and children'. Wherever it came from, *snollygoster* – defined in 1895 as 'a fellow who wants office, regardless of party, platform or principles' – is now more useful than ever.

11 SEPTEMBER

Spifflicated

The short-story master O. Henry was born William Sydney Porter on this day in 1862, and he it was who coined the term *spifflicated* to mean 'drunk'. In 'Memoirs of a Yellow Dog' (1906), the canine narrator, who is taken out for walks only very reluctantly by the man of the household, asks the dog from across the hall why his master always comes back from their walks so cheerful. 'Why, he uses Nature's Own Remedy,' replies the neighbouring dog. 'He gets *spifflicated* ... By the time we've been in eight saloons he don't care whether the thing on the end of his line is a dog or a catfish.'

The verb *spifflicate* – 'probably a purely fanciful forma-tion', comments the *OED* drily – had already existed (since 1749) to mean 'defeat', 'harm', 'crush', or 'destroy', but Henry made the meaning of drunkenness stick. So raise a glass to him next time you're in the process of getting *spifflicated*.

12 SEPTEMBER

Bibliobibuli

The American satirist H. L. Mencken was born on this day in 1880, and though a learned man and highly prolific author, he reckoned some of his fellows needed to get out more. 'There are people who read too much: the *bibliobibuli*,' he wrote in a fragment later published in *Minority Report: H. L. Mencken's Notebooks* (1956), combining the Greek for 'book' (*biblios*) with the Latin for 'fond of drinking' (*bibulus*). 'I know some who are constantly drunk on books, as other men are drunk on whiskey or religion. They wander through this most diverting and stimulating of worlds in a haze, seeing nothing and hearing nothing.' To which one might respond by reminding him of what T. S. Eliot wrote: 'Human kind / Cannot bear very much reality.'

Altiloquence

One who speaks more grandly than the occasion demands is perhaps guilty of *altiloquence*, or as you might say 'high-flown language' (literally, from the Latin). Dr Johnson defines it as 'pompous language', and others follow, calling it pedantic or affected.

But the word's first appearance in English is not disapproving: it comes in a translation of the *Essays* by Michel de Montaigne, who died on this day in 1592, where the great French writer celebrates the styles of different European tongues. 'Every language hath its *Genius* and inseparable Form ... The Tuscan *altiloquence*, the *Venus* of the French, the sharp state of the Spanish, the strong significancy of the Dutch ...' One might add today, perhaps, that the problem is not that there is too much refined speech and writing, but rather the opposite. So let's have one cheer for *altiloquence*: when they go low, we'll go high.

Malefic

What is *malefic* is baleful or evil in influence, from the Latin for 'ill-doing'. Such are noxious stellar influences in old astrology, or practices of black magic, the *malefic* arts. Secular crimes and social problems, too, can be *malefic*, as can wizards, and especially witches.

Apropos of which, in her seminal *Sexual Politics* (1972), the American feminist writer Kate Millett, born on this day in 1934, argues that Victorian literature evinces fantasies of 'feminine evil' contrasted with virtuous womanhood. In Rossetti and Swinburne, however, 'even the eternal need to vent disapproval on the *malefic* woman begins to disappear' – but only because the figure of the 'bitch goddess' becomes something to worship rather than recoil from. The trope of the *malefic* woman, meanwhile, is still very much with us.

15 September

Roily

The novelist James Fenimore Cooper, author of *The Last of the Mohicans*, was born on this day in 1789; among his more obscure achievements is being the first writer cited by the *OED* to use the word *roily*, in 1823. It means 'muddy' or 'cloudy', from the sense of the verb *roil*, 'to stir up water'. But its application is not limited to describing rivers or glasses of beer; a later scholar described 'a *roily* flood of historical fiction' erupting across the American scene at the turn of the twentieth century, and a *New Yorker* writer of the present millennium described a certain baseball game as *roily*.

Puzzlingly, the close synonym *riley* (apparently from 'to rile up') can be applied to muddy water and also to irritable people, or even, in Oregon, bad-tempered cows, but *roily* has not so far crossed the barrier from inanimate fluids to sensible organisms. There are certainly enough *roily* people around to recommend its adoption.

16 September

Logomachy

People have always loved to dispute the proper meaning and usage of words, which pedantic entertainment we might ennoble, on International Dictionary Day, with the name *logomachy*. From the Greek for 'word' and 'battle', it is defined by Dr Johnson as 'A contention in words; a contention about words'. He cites the historian James Howell: 'Forced terms of art did much puzzle sacred theology with distinctions, cavils, quiddities, and so transformed her to a mere kind of sophistry and *logomachy*.'

For most of its history, *logomachy* has been employed as a putdown ('vain logomachies', 'mere logomachy'), but it can also, more relaxingly, mean any kind of word game. At the 1874 Cincinnati Industrial Exposition, which ran during the whole of this month, the prize of best new parlour game was won by a children's spelling game using alphabet cards called ... *Logomachy*.

The word's secondary meaning, a battle conducted in words (i.e., a debate) is defined with exemplary gloom by Ambrose Bierce: 'A kind of contest in which, the vanquished being unconscious of defeat, the victor is denied the reward of success.'

Scrutation

Many modern sources will tell you that *scrutation* is just an old variant of *scrutiny*, and means the same thing, but the truth is more interesting. *Scrutation* describes a minute examination or inquiry, a thorough analysis, and supposedly derives at length from the Latin *scruta*, meaning 'rubbish': so *scrutation* is such a thorough search that it even looks through the detritus. While *scrutiny* derives from the same root, its original sense in English is political, and means the formal counting of votes in an assembly. Its sense then widened to denote a critical inquiry, or a close staring, or latterly the act of holding politicians to account.

But *scrutation* still carries an extra sense of thorough-going investigation that *scrutiny* does not quite evoke. One who practises such *scrutation* may be termed a *scrutator*, and a Big Brother-type figure who surveils all in his domain is a Central Scrutinizer, according to Frank Zappa's concept album *Joe's Garage*, the first volume of which was released on this day in 1979, and which still warrants minute aural *scrutation*.

18 September

Stammel

One of the joys of Samuel Johnson's *Dictionary* is coming across entries that clearly caught him in a bad mood. Such is *stammel*, for which the definition reads in its entirety: 'Of this word I know not the meaning.' Dear Doctor, you had one job. He does, however, cite an exchange in a work by Ben Jonson: 'Redhood, the first that doth appear / In *stammel*.' 'Scarlet is too dear.' If you are guessing from this context that *stammel* might be a shade of red, you are correct.

Originally, *stammel* was a kind of coarse woollen cloth (from the Latin, in a roundabout way, for 'warp threads'), and since such material was usually dyed a scarlet-like red (but, as Jonson relates, not so expensively), it came to denote that colour too. Henry Cockeram's 1623 *Dictionary* speaks of 'Cutchoneale ... wherewith *Stammell* is died' – in other words cochineal, the dye made from the eponymous insects that yields colours from carmine to scarlet – though a later writer suggests that berries can do the job too. But even Homer nods, so let us not be too hard on Samuel Johnson, whose birthday it is today: he emerged blinking into the world in 1709:

Blatteration

If you ever encounter someone indulging in senseless babble, or as modern Londoners say 'chatting breeze', you might accuse them of *blatteration*. The verb *to blatter* (*OED*: 'to speak or prate volubly') is known from 1533: you can *blatter* intransitively (prate on and on), or you can *blatter* specific notions. The practice of *blatteration* follows in 1656, when Blount's *Glossographia* defines it as 'vain-babbling, flattering in speech'.

The original recording sessions for Bob Dylan's album *Blood on the Tracks*, which includes the song 'Idiot Wind', were finished on this day in 1974: like *babbling* itself, *blatteration* has the virtue of onomatopoeia, suggesting the sound of someone's lips and teeth flapping uselessly in the idiot wind.

Constult

One of the advantages of the digital age is that it makes it so much easier for people to *constult*, or be stupid together (Latin *con–*, 'with', plus *stultus*, 'fool'). Writers have not resisted the temptation to use it in conjunction with the more sober verb it might at first glance be confused with: so John Taylor in 1630: 'Some English gentlemen with him consulted / And he as nat'rally with them *constulted*.'

So too John Gauden, the Bishop of Worcester, who died on this day in 1662. In a 1659 sermon at St Paul's Cathedral, he said of timid physicians: 'If they dare not own, or cannot attack either the source and head of the disease, or the streams and potency of it, [to] what [purpose] do they meet and sit and consult (or rather *constult*) together? They had as good cast their caps, as thus lay their heads together, when they have no mind to do the work, nor courage to go through with the cure.' A modern cynic might follow Gauden's example and suggest that, in the wider world, much of what passes for consultation is, too, *constultation*.

Cachinnation

We have all encountered someone who laughs too loudly and too long, cackling like a demented thing at the slightest provocation: such a person is guilty of *cachinnation*. From the Latin *cacchinare*, meaning the same thing – evidently such people were around in ancient Rome too – it has been used lamentingly in English since 1623.

The word is employed with aplomb by Sir Walter Scott, who died on this day in 1832. In his novel *Guy Mannering* (1815), the old Laird is described thus: 'It is true, he never laughed, or joined in the laugh which his own simplicity afforded – nay, it is said he never laughed but once in his life; and on that memorable occasion his landlady miscarried, partly through surprise at the event itself, and partly from terror at the hideous grimaces which attended this unusual *cachinnation*.' Truly a frightful sound, however rarely heard.

22 September

Entregent

English lacks a single word for general 'social interaction' or 'small talk', where *conversation* might be too specific – or at least it does now, since we stopped employing the classy term *entregent*. This was a straight steal from Norman French, literally meaning 'between people' (*entre gens*), and possessing a quality *entregent* was the sign of a classy person. The politician Philip Dormer Stanhope, Lord Chesterfield, born on this day in 1694, advised his son in a letter how to flirt with women: he should be 'exceedingly respectful, but at the same time easy and unembarrassed. Your chit-chat or *entregent* with them neither can, nor ought to be very solid; but you should take care to turn and dress up your trifles prettily, and make them, every now and then, convey indirectly some little piece of flattery.'

John Donne, Jr., the son of the poet, pointed out in his edition of the correspondence of the courtier Sir Toby Matthew that the art of letter-writing was 'the *Entregent* of absent Persons; it is the solace and satisfaction of suspended minds; it is the communication of everlist'ning friends'. Postings on social media today, too, are the *entregent* of absent persons, and if we so described them there might be a pleasant outbreak of civility.

Flexanimous

What is *flexanimous* is literally, from the Latin, 'mind-bending', and so highly persuasive. This can be meant positively – so Thomas Adams, who was ordained on this day in 1604 and is, on one scholar's assessment, 'one of the more considerable buried literary talents of the seventeenth century', refers in one of his sermons to St Peter as 'that *flexanimous* Preacher, whose Pulpit is in Heaven'. But it can also have a negative connotation, of bullying or crafty persuasion, as when an earlier preacher (of Earthly pulpit) wrote that faith 'stands not without doors as a Mendicant [begging] *Flexanimous* persuader, but enters into the closets of the heart'.

A useful twist is that, according to Thomas Blount, *flexanimous* can also denote 'a mind easily bent or turned'. And so the *flexanimous* might be led astray by the *flexanimous*, in this age as in all the others.

24 September

Mundivagant

The footloose traveller or indulger in wanderlust is one who is *mundivagant*, a serious term for 'wandering through the world' (Dr Johnson). Straightforwardly derived from the Latin for 'world' and 'wander', it was taken up in the nineteenth century for those writers with a taste for wry pomposity: a writer for the *Gentleman's Magazine* in 1803, for example, pleonastically described 'A *Mundivagant* mendicant, nay, a cosmopolite, who was ... clad in hermetical weeds'. The *mundivagant* person, then, is also a *cosmopolitan* (Greek, 'citizen of the world'), and may positively relish the accusation of being a citizen of nowhere, or the transcendent state of *nullibiety* (Dr Johnson: 'the state of being nowhere'). History, after all, celebrates its *mundivagant* heroes, including the first Englishman to reach Japan, the sailor William Adams, who was baptized on this day in 1564.

In the twentieth century, *mundivagant* was mainly applied humorously to American politicians whose whereabouts at critical votes could not be established; you might suspect that if they really did wander the world more often, citizens might see an improvement in policy.

Abruption

The breaking off of some action, or the interruption of speech, is called *abruption*, from the Latin for 'to break away'. In Shakespeare's *Troilus and Cressida*, the lovers are talking when Cressida breaks off thus: 'The gods grant – O, my lord!' To which Troilus responds: 'What should they grant? What makes this pretty *abruption*?'

In *The Devil's Dictionary*, Ambrose Bierce includes the word sardonically: 'Dr Johnson said of a certain work that the ideas were "concatenated without *abruption*". In deference to that great authority we have given the word a place.' Yet it was not so obscure then, and went on to find especial employment in twentieth-century medicine, where it denotes the tearing away of some tissue. It might still be useful to discuss whether there is *abruption* in the flow of thoughts, conversation, or even music. As the American music critic Michael Steinberg wrote in 1995, a certain composer 'juxtaposes the most disparate musical elements and moves by startling *abruptions*'. That he does; so on this day let us celebrate the birth, in 1906, of Dmitri Shostakovich.

Latitation

The hibernating season for North American bears begins around now. Should you wish to imitate their enviable example and hide from the world, you will be in a state of *latitation*, 'a lurking' (Cockeram) from the Latin for 'to lie hidden'. Nothing wrong with that now and again, unless the *latitation* is designed to escape justice: in Roman law, attempting to refuse a summons by latitation rendered you liable to being forcibly wrenched from your house. Even to dodge behind a column to avoid a creditor was considered *latitation*, according to the classical scholar Henry John Roby in his 1902 study *Roman Private Law*. So a carefree *latitation* is best enjoyed, as bears know too, after one has put one's affairs in order.

Habnab

When things seem to be chaotic and unpredictable – in other words, all the time – it is useful to have to hand the word *habnab*. Dr Johnson says it means 'At random; at the mercy of chance; without any rule or certainty of effect', and explains it as a version of 'hap ne hap', meaning 'let it happen or not', though the *OED* suggests rather that 'hab or nab' means 'to have or have not'; the upshot is still that *habnab* means 'any which way'.

As illustration, Johnson quotes Samuel Butler's satirical poem *Hudibras*, in which the quack astrologer Sidrophel attempts to demonstrate his skills: 'He circles draws and squares, / With cyphers, astral characters; / Then looks 'em o'er to understand 'em, / Although set down *habnab* at random.' Butler was buried on this day in 1680, and the world's affairs have hardly become less *habnab* since.

Fatiferous

No more forbidding word for 'forbiddingness', perhaps, can be conjured than the doomy-sounding *fatiferous*, from the Latin for 'fate-bringing'. Dr Johnson defines it laconically as meaning 'Deadly; mortal; destructive', and so it has been used when applied to snakes and military occupations. It was particularly popular, perhaps for nothing more than its impressive sonority, among American lawyers and doctors around the turn of the twentieth century. (One of the latter tribe refers darkly in 1899 to 'the *fatiferous* thought that Brooklyn never will produce specialists' of the calibre to be found in Manhattan.)

Ann Julia Hatton, an actress and popular novelist (publishing as Ann of Swansea) of the nineteenth century, has a doctor lament in one of her novels that, despite his valiant efforts, a violent fever has proved *fatiferous*, i.e. fatal, to his patient. On this day in 1838 she wrote 'Farewell Lines' in verse to her friend Dr Douglas Cohen, knowing that her own present illness would soon itself prove *fatiferous*.

Antonomasia

If one refers to 'the President' instead of using the name of the present holder of that office, or to 'the Redeemer' instead of Jesus, one is practising the ancient rhetorical art of *antonomasia*. From the Greek for 'to name instead', *antonomasia* originally (from 1553) meant replacing a proper name with a descriptive epithet: so, in bygone times, *the philosopher* always meant Aristotle, while *the poet* denoted Homer. Within half a century, however, it had acquired a symmetrically opposite sense: now it could also denote the generic use of any proper name to cover a whole class of things. So to call any wise man a Solomon, or any evil man a Hitler, is also a species of *antonomasia*.

Humans love to play around with names so much that *antonomasia* is itself far more common than the name for it. To sum up: to call *Macbeth* 'the Scottish play' is *antonomasia* in the first sense, while to call any ballpoint pen a biro is to use the second, though the Hungarian-Argentine inventor László Bíró, who gave his name to that brand of writing implement – and was born on this day in 1899 – probably wouldn't mind.

Termagant

In the medieval French heroic poems, *Tervagan* is the name for one of the three 'idols' supposedly worshipped by 'pagans' (Muslims), the other two being Mahound and Apollin. The origin of the name Tervagan is uncertain, though it has been interpreted as meaning 'thrice-wandering' and so the Moon (which, mythically, has three personalities). In any case *Tervagan* mutated, as it passed into English, to *termagant*, which from the early sixteenth century could now mean any aggressive, overbearing person, or violent bully. It is used in this way by Shakespeare, in whose *Henry IV, Part 1* Falstaff refers to Douglas as 'that hot termagant Scot'.

There followed later an unfortunate tradition of reserving *termagant* for bad-tempered women, though male characters – from Cupid to Donald Duck – could still be called *termagant* by those who valued equality of insult. It was, too, reportedly a favourite term of abuse, applied to his fellow men, of the Australian politician Kim Beazley, Sr., who was born on this day in 1917.

OCTOBER

1 October

Sprunking

When you check in a mirror and adjust your appearance before photographing yourself, you are *sprunking* – a word that, pronounced with appropriate care, will doubtless carry a full cargo of lip-pursing disapproval if applied to the activities of others. It is first recorded in written English thanks to the poet Mary Evelyn, born on this day in 1665. In her posthumously published book, *Mundus Muliebris, or, The Ladies Dressing-Room Unlock'd, and Her Toilets Spread: In Burlesque; together with the Fop-Dictionary, compiled for the Use of the Fair Sex* (1690), Evelyn writes that *sprunking* is 'a Dutch term for Pruning, Tiffing, Trimming, and setting out, by the Glass or Pocket Miroir'. (Such a mirror itself is called, marvellously, a *sprunking-glass*.)

The *OED* notes the Dutch word *pronken* ('to be vain','to dress up'), and considers that the preceding *s* is 'excrescent', i.e. was added for no meaningful reason. It also provides a wonderful later use, in a historical novel of 1827: 'He offered his *sprunking-glass* to the disordered baronet.' If anyone really needs a *sprunking-glass*, it is surely disordered baronets.

2 October

Funest

The peerless American poet Wallace Stevens was born on this day in 1879, so let us celebrate here one of the beautiful archaisms he was wont to resurrect. What is *funest* is not most fun, but rather (pronounced FEWnest) derives from the Latin for 'funeral', and so means 'deathly', 'portending doom', or *fatiferous* (see 28 September).

Stevens, as often was his habit, employs it for comic effect in his poem 'On the Manner of Addressing Clouds' (1921): 'Gloomy grammarians in golden gowns ... / Funest philosophers and ponderers, / Their evocations are the speech of clouds.' And so, in a way, were his.

3 OCTOBER

Cosmodelyte

The former NASA engineer and Bible student Edgar C. Whisenant predicted the beginning of World War Three on this day in 1988, which would in turn usher in the Christian Rapture, when true believers and the righteous dead would all be raised up to heaven. This prediction had already been revised after the Rapture had mysteriously failed to occur the previous month; when it didn't happen on this day either, Whisenant changed his prediction to 30 September 1989, which must have been a shame for the four and a half million people who had bought his book entitled *88 Reasons Why the Rapture Will Be in 1988*. Still, such apocalyptic thinkers do not have the monopoly on being *cosmodelytes*: a lovely obsolete word for those who are frightened about the state of the world. As Thomas Blount's 1656 dictionary *Glossographia*, at that time the largest yet compiled, explained, *cosmodelyte* is formed from the Greek *cosmos* ('the world') and *deilos* (either 'afraid' or 'miserable'), and so means 'one fearful of the world, or a worldly wretch'. There is still no shortage of either.

4 OCTOBER

Overmorrow

In some ways, English has become less efficient over the centuries, with perfectly good single words for things having been replaced by clumsy phrases. Why not, then, revive *overmorrow*, instead of always having to trudge through the phrase 'the day after tomorrow'? Like *yesterneve* (see 6 October), this is both easier to pronounce and more satisfying than the alternative. It probably comes from the German *übermorgen*, literally meaning the same thing, but mysteriously has not been much in evidence since the sixteenth century. Its first recorded appearance is in the first complete Bible in English: that translated by Myles Coverdale, the printing of which was completed on this day in 1535.

Jobbernowl

A vivid and evocative insult that has not been worn out by overuse is always useful, so let us repopularize *jobbernowl*. This means simply 'idiot', 'numbskull', or 'blockhead', but why? The *OED* points to the French *jobard* meaning a particularly naive or gullible person, and *Larousse* traces this to Middle French *jobe*, which derives from the biblical Job himself. But Dr Johnson has an alternative etymology: 'most probably from *jobbe*, Flemish, dull, and *nowl*, *knol*, Saxon, a head.' Certainly, in English *jobbernowl* can also be used to refer to the head of an idiot, as a magazine writer did on this day in 1709: 'Alas! poor Numphs [idiot], thy *Jobbernole* / Seems scarce informed by a Soul.'

The truth of its origin may be unrecoverable, but there is certainly something satisfying about *jobbernowl*, perhaps because we can't help hearing *jowls* and *nobs* with interchanged consonants. In fact the word has never fallen totally out of use. In 1991, a writer for the London *Times* expostulated: 'The capitalist system ... seems to be organized, led and operated exclusively by numbskulls, dunces ... wallies and *jobbernowls*.' This diagnosis, we might agree, remains all too current.

Yesterneve

Why go to all the trouble of saying 'yesterday evening' when there exists a fine, single English word for just that? *Yesterneve* occurs in Aelfric's *Lives of the Saints* (c. 1000), and on up until *The Romance of William of Palerne* (1375), but thereafter soon vanishes from the record, as though people, in the grip of some mass amnesia, no longer needed to refer to the evening of the day before.

We know all this because of the tireless editing work done on such early manuscripts by the philologist Walter William Skeat, who died on this day in 1912. He was also the author of an important *Etymological Dictionary* (1879), and is said to have been the first Cambridge professor to ride a bicycle. Let us revive *yesterneve* in his honour.

Paramnesia

This word was first coined in French (*paramnésie*) by the nineteenth-century doctor Jacques Lordat, describing the difficulties with speech he experienced following a stroke: he gave the term *paramnesia* to a misremembering of which words went with which things. ('When I wanted to ask for a book,' he relates, 'I said the word "handkerchief".')

But its modern sense was introduced by the German psychiatrist Emil Kraepelin, who died on this day in 1926. He used the term *paramnesia* (its shortened prefix *para*– carrying the sense of 'associated with, but separate from, *amnesia* proper') to cover various errors in memory, including what he called *identifying paramnesia*, where one seems to remember that what one is currently experiencing has happened identically, in all respects, before. And so *paramnesia* became the technical name for what we also know as *déjà vu*. I can assure the reader that this entry does not recur elsewhere in the book.

Uranomania

Such is the variety of human delusion that there is a dictionary's worth of –*mania* words to describe peculiar beliefs; but one of the prettiest is *uranomania*, which is the false conviction that one is of divine origin. Lest you think it a mere nonceword, be advised that its first appearance is in the *National Medical Dictionary* (1890), compiled by the American surgeon and librarian John Shaw Billings. *Uranomania* is there described as 'monomania involving the idea of a divine or celestial origin or connection; a species of megalomania'. (Uranus, the planet, was named after one of the Greek gods; but the Greek *ouranos* also means 'of the heavens' generally, and so the English prefix *urano–* is used to mean 'divine' or 'celestial'.)

In a 1920 history of the Tsars, satisfyingly entitled *The Imperial Orgy*, by the decadent American writer Edgar Saltus – who was born on this day in 1855 – it is written of the assassinated Nicholas II: 'Commonsense might have preserved him. But in his case ... commonsense would have been abnormal. Instead was a derangement, clinically known as *uranomania*. A dwarf fancied himself divine.' Those not of a religious persuasion, indeed, might suspect that the course of world history before and since has been profoundly altered by a handful of individuals suffering from *uranomania*.

Gudgeon

A *gudgeon* is a little fish (*Gobio fluviatilis*), which is 'of pleasant taste', so someone records in 1620, and which anglers often use for bait to catch larger fishes. It is not the cleverest of fishes; indeed, remarks a seventeenth-century gentleman's manual, gudgeons 'are Fish of eager bite and soonest deceived'. Which is why a *gudgeon* also came to be used to describe a credulous, gullible person. As the artist and socialite Mary Granville wrote to her sister in 1728, responding to reports of a man's romantic interest in her: 'You are a mere wag, sister, to think London ladies such *gudgeons* as to bite at anything.'

This sense is first recorded as appearing in *The Discoverie of Witchcraft* (1584), an important work of sceptical history, which argues that black magic is impossible because words cannot alter the world: its humane author was the engineer and scholar Reginald Scott, who died on this day in 1599. Remarking on the practice of inserting needles into a wax figurine of someone you wish to harm, he judges: 'They would do no harm, were it not to make fools, and catch *gudgins*.' The same can be said of cults and quackeries to this day.

Cepphick

The English scientist Henry Cavendish, born on this day in 1731, became in 1766 the first person to recognize the existence of hydrogen as an individual gas, which he called 'inflammable air'. (It was christened *hydrogen* for 'water-making' by Antoine Lavoisier.) It could well be described as a *cepphick* (pronounced SEFFiK) element, were this lovely word still current. It derives from the Latin *cepphicus*, meaning 'extremely light' (as hydrogen is the lightest element), and Thomas Blount says *cepphick* is possible in English to mean 'very light, trifling, of no estimation'. If we wished to speak metaphorically, rather than only of things with very little physical mass, we should want the word *cepphick* for very many cultural manifestations of the present, too.

11 OCTOBER

Agerasia

A person who looks very good for their age is one blessed with the quality of *agerasia* (pronounced adjerAYzha). This has nothing to do with the word *age* itself, but comes from the Greek word for 'eternal youth', formed from the negating prefix *a–*, plus *geras*, 'old age'.

It first appears in the new 1706 edition of Edward Phillips's *The New World of Words*, which was revised and enlarged by John Kersey, who completed his apprenticeship in printing on this day in 1680. Kersey went on, among other things, to translate Plutarch and to expand Phillips's dictionary by adding, as he said, '20,000 hard words in arts and sciences', including *agerasia*, defined as 'a vigorous old age'. Sources do not record the exact date of his death, so it is possible to hope John Kersey enjoyed one himself.

12 OCTOBER

Anfractuous

What is *anfractuous*, says Dr Johnson, is 'winding; mazy; full of turnings and winding passages'. From the Latin *anfractus*, 'a bending', this lovely word – one of those that seem to mime their own meaning – has been applied to streets, mountain passages, and the fleshy whorls of the ear, among other things, including actual labyrinths. Life itself, moreover, could hope for few more accurate epithets than *anfractuous*. The English poet and theologian Henry More, born on this day in 1614, has a character in his *Divine Dialogues* (1668) fear for the future, 'So intricate, so *anfractuous*, so unsearchable are the ways of Providence.'

Rudyard Kipling, meanwhile, employs the word as an amusing metaphor in his 1932 story 'Aunt Ellen', where a young policeman remarks: 'If Police Sergeants have been up all night on duty they appreciate a run in the fresh air before turning in. If they've been hoicked out of bed, ad hoc, they're apt to be *anfractuous*.' One knows how they feel.

13 October

Pumpkinification

The Roman emperor Claudius died by poisoning, possibly at the hands of his wife Agrippina, on this day in 54 CE. Shortly afterwards, his successor and great-nephew Nero, along with the Senate, officially pronounced him to be a god. Some were not so impressed, however, and Seneca the Younger wrote a satire about Claudius called the *Apocolocyntosis*. This is a play on the Greek (and later English) word *apotheosis*, which literally means 'becoming a god'; but here Seneca writes of how Claudius became a pumpkin. *Pumpkinification*, then, means any 'extravagant or absurdly uncritical glorification' (*OED*), and so serves as a more mocking general version of *hagiography*: as one waspish reviewer wrote in 1904, the biography he was reading was 'not an apotheosis, but a *pumpkinification* of the Emperor William II'. Do we live now in an age where *pumpkinification* is the norm?

Isagoge

Those who might feel embarrassed to admit that they are reading a Bluffer's Guide or other basic introduction to some subject might like instead to say, in more highfalutin manner, that they are immersed in an *isagoge* (pronounced eyesaGOjee). This word is formed from the Greek for 'to lead in', and first attested in 1652; its pedagogical flavour is apt for this, World Standards Day, celebrating the harmonization of technical and scientific standards around the globe.

The word *isagoge* itself was still current in academic circles in the late nineteenth century, as evident from its appearance in the 1860 dictionary *An Expository Lexicon of the Terms, Ancient and Modern, in Medical and General Science*: '*Isagoge* ... Term for an introduction', especially to a medical subject. If anyone asks, you may also explain that you are currently embarking on an *isagogic* study, which is likely to impress annyoing inquirers into a pleasant silence.

15 OCTOBER

Yex

Yex, or *yesk*, is an extremely old word. It was already of eight hundred years' vintage when the Scottish poet Allan Ramsay, born on this day in 1684, employed it in his touching 'Elegy on Maggy Johnston'. 'We us'd to drink and rant,' he remembers, 'Until we did baith [both] glow'r and gaunt [yawn], / And pish and spew, and *yesk* and maunt [stammer].' They sound like most agreeable boozing sessions. Anyway, *yesk* is here used to describe a familiar effect of alcohol. As Blount's *Glossographia* explains: 'To *Yex*, is that we do, when we have the Hicket or Hick up.' But that sense is only recorded since 1400; going back further, to *yex* was to sob. The word, according to the *OED*, comes from the Old English *geocsian*, and is onomatopoeic. And so hiccuping and sobbing share an etymological root, just as too much of one might lead to the other.

Noceur

If you are an inveterate nocturnal reveller, you may be termed a *noceur*. In French, *les noces* are usually marriage celebrations, but *nocer* can mean 'to party', whether or not anyone is getting married, and so a *noceur* is a reveller. In English, however, a *noceur* is particularly rakish and dissolute: its first recorded use, in 1908, was to note that such a person 'is only too pleased to show himself in the company of some well-known "horizontale"', the latter being a French euphemism for 'courtesan'.

Rather winningly, the English painter Sir William Rothenstein, in his 1931 memoir entitled *Men & Memories*, recalls of his Paris salad days: 'I didn't care for the poets' cafés – they were too crowded and noisy; and though I could, on occasion, sit up most of the night, I was not a *noceur*. Wilde said of me that I was like those dreadful public-houses in London – punctually at midnight all the lights went out of my face.' It confers nonetheless some literary immortality to have drunk with, and been fondly teased by, Oscar Wilde himself, who was born on this day in 1854.

Diple

The *diple* is the mark >, named thus after the Greek for 'double line'. It was used by classical authors as a marginal mark to indicate that something was missing, or that something needed correcting, and may still be so used today, so why not give it its proper name? It is pleasant, after all, to have another name for this sign when it is not being used mathematically to mean 'greater than'.

The *diple*'s first printed use in this algebraic way (as what we now call an 'inequality sign') was in the posthumously published papers of the English mathematician Thomas Harriot. He was also a fine astronomer, having observed the moon through a telescope before Galileo did, and on this day in 1610 he began a groundbreaking five-month observation of the moons of Jupiter.

Antithalian

One who is opposed to festivities of all kinds, a dour and Scroogey sort of person, may be termed *antithalian*. It was a word casually dropped by Thomas Love Peacock – born on this day in 1785 – in his wonderful pastiche of the Gothic romance and of the Romantics themselves, *Nightmare Abbey*. Herein, one Miss Celinda Toobad is described proudly by her father as being 'altogether as gloomy and *antithalian* a young lady as Mr Glowry himself could desire for the future mistress of Nightmare Abbey'.

The Greek figure of Thalia was the muse of comedy and the grace of parties, so anyone who dislikes both – for instance, the kind of person who, in modern cities, moves into a new apartment near a famous old music venue or bar, and then promptly begins to complain about the noise – may properly be termed *antithalian*, and much else besides.

Ingannation

Ingannation is trickery or deception, from the Italian *ingannare* to deceive, and it is used splendidly by the doctor and Renaissance man Thomas Browne in his 1646 work *Pseudodoxia Epidemica*, a compendium of false ideas with a title that one might now translate as *An Epidemic of Fake News*. Therein, Browne (who died on this day in 1682) takes aim at the duncery of such people as quack doctors, astrologers, fortune tellers, and the like, but he really gets motoring on the subject of politicians, among whose vices, he says, are an 'inability to resist ... trivial *ingannations* from others'.

Browne's book was a hit and went through several reprintings over the next few decades. In the sixth edition *ingannations* was quietly changed to 'deceptions', perhaps because no one, after all, had really understood it. In a grumpy mood, Dr Johnson later called *ingannation* 'a word neither used nor necessary', in which case one might reasonably ask why he included it in his *Dictionary*.

20 October

Concinnity

If something is harmonious, beautifully proportioned, and so forth, then it has the quality of *concinnity*. This beautiful word comes from the Latin *concinnus*, 'well put together', and has been used in English to mean 'elegance' (of writing style), 'musical concord', and even the admirable design of Sicilian money. The English Catholic theologian John Sergeant, who was buried on this day in 1707, wrote in his confidently titled book *Solid Philosophy Asserted* (1697) that mere definitions of philosophical terms were useless; the trick was to 'to polish our Notions, and bring them to Exactness and *Concinnity*'.

The Latin word itself seems to derive, pleasingly enough, from *cinnus*, a blended drink of grain and wine. Next time you drink a good cocktail, then, be sure to praise the *concinnity* of the bartender's work.

21 OCTOBER

Paedocracy

Democracy is only one of many potential forms of government, including *dodecarchy* – a rule of twelve people, as was tried for a time in ancient Egypt – but one unlikely to catch on is *paedocracy*, 'rule by children'. Too much power too young can go to one's head, as it seems to have done in the case of King Charles VI of France, who died on this day in 1422. He inherited the throne at the tender age of 11, and for a while he was known as *le bien-Aimé* (the Beloved), until his erratic behaviour — as a young man, he attacked and killed several of his own knights on a hunt — led him to be redubbed *le Fou* (the mad).

The inadvisability of paedocracy hasn't stopped the word popping up regularly since its first recorded use, by the Reverend James Noyes in 1647. Noyes was not, mind you, recommending government by children; rather, he was complaining that some people in authority were 'unseasonable, ignorant, youthful', and so, he lamented: 'This is a *Pedocracy* as well as a Democracy.' From then on, *paedocracy* (or *paedarchy*, meaning the same thing) was used sarcastically for either groups of immature politicians, or an over-indulgent way of running a family according to the wishes of the children – about which eyebrows were already being raised in 1927, there being little new under the sun.

Brumal

In the French Revolutionary Calendar, today was the first day of the second month, known as *brumaire* – from *brume*, the modern French for 'fog'. English, though, borrowed the root earlier: the middle French *brumal* meant more generally 'belonging to winter' or 'wintry' (Latin *brumalis*, ultimately from a shorthand way of saying 'the shortest day'). This was transported across the Channel in the sixteenth century, and has since served as a poetic and somehow onomatopoeic adjective for the cold season. As one writer put it in 1813: 'Dark indeed are the *brumal* days that have no sunshine.' Wrap up warm.

Epicaricacy

It is often said that English has no equivalent of the German word *Schadenfreude*, but happily it does, if one so little used that even the *OED* neglects to mention it. But *epicharikaky* is to be found in Nathan Bailey's 1763 *An Universal Etymological English Dictionary*, where it is defined straightforwardly as 'a Joy at the Misfortunes of others'. Indeed the word is ancient Greek for 'joy upon evil', and Robert Burton's *Anatomy of Melancholy* uses it in Greek to mean the same thing and its inverse: 'a compound affection of joy and hate, when we rejoice at other men's mischief, and are grieved at their prosperity'. (The compound Greek word itself first appears in Aristotle's *Nicomachean Ethics*.) *Epicharikaky* is thus of much earlier vintage than *Schadenfreude* itself, which is first mentioned in English only in 1852.

Of late, surprisingly, this buried gem it has enjoyed something of a renaissance in the modernized spelling *epicaricacy*. On this day in 2013, it was reported that researchers from Princeton University had concluded that feeling gleeful about an envied person's misfortune was a universal human trait. Since *epicaricacy* is such a common feeling, we might as well have our own word for it.

Debacchation

The lawyer and pamphleteer William Prynne, who died on this day in 1669, fulminated (he was quite the fulminator) about people who 'defile' saints' holidays 'with most foolish vanities, most impure pollutions, most wicked *debacchations*, and sacrilegious execrations'. One has to say those parties do sound fun: particular the *debacchations*, or acts in honour of the Greek god Bacchus, aka Dionysus: patron of wine, fertility, and good times (as also in *bacchanals*).

Such was Prynne's style of moralizing in his splendidly dyspeptic book, to give it a truncated title, *Histrio-Mastix, The Players Scourge; or, Actors Tragœdie . . . Wherein it is largely evidenced . . . that popular stageplayes . . . are sinfull, heathenish, lewde, ungodly spectacles*, and so forth (1633). Prynne herein denounced (among other things) the appearance of women on the stage, but when his pamphlet was printed, Queen Henrietta Maria was herself acting in a masque at Court. Prynne was brought up on charges of sedition, but acquitted – justly so. As William Lamont puts it unimprovably in his entry for Prynne in the *Oxford Dictionary of National Biography*: '*Histriomastix* is a crime against literature, not against the state.'

25 October

Amphibology

Something that is ambiguous is an example of *amphibology*, from the Greek *amphi–* ('around', 'on both sides of', hence *amphitheatre*), plus *bolos* ('throw'), and so literally 'to be attacked on both sides'. In *Troilus and Criseyde* by Geoffrey Chaucer – who died on this day in 1400 – we are warned: 'For goddes speken in *amphibologies*, / And for o sooth, they tellen twenty lies.' Much later, the economist and logician William Stanley Jevons wrote in 1870: 'The fallacy of *Amphibology* consists in an ambiguous grammatical structure of a sentence which produces misconception.' It can be difficult to avoid perpetrating *amphibology*, can't it?

You might meanwhile ask why this word seems so close to *amphibious*, which is the correct question, because that comes similarly from the Greek for 'life on both sides', and so means 'living both on land and in water'. Perhaps a person who is comfortable with *amphibologies* is one who is logically amphibious.

Agathokakological

From the Greek *agathos*, 'good', and *kakos*, 'evil', this is a handy term to describe anything that is a mixture of good and evil, from the entire world downwards. In 1834, the poet Robert Southey wrote of the mischief caused by people who misused words and so 'blundered into heresies and erroneous assertions of every kind'. However, he continues, 'There may be an opposite fault; for indeed upon the *agathokakological* globe there are opposite qualities always to be found in parallel degrees ... A man may dwell upon words till he becomes at length a mere precisian in speech. He may think of their meaning till he loses sight of all meaning, and they appear as dark and mysterious to him as chaos and outer night.'

This is a salutary warning to anyone who dares to compose a book about words. It's nice to think that Southey's deployment of *agathokakological* here is itself a little joke, given that he is about to write about word-fetishism. One might expect this word to have fallen into utter *desuetude* (see 10 February), yet it reappeared on this day in 2008, when a Melbourne newspaper reported on the opinion that humans are '*agathokakological*, which is the condition of being equal parts good and evil'. Indeed, until all evil is removed from the world, this word will have its use.

27 OCTOBER

Widdershins

In his poem 'Do You Not Father Me' (1936), Dylan Thomas – who was born on this day in 1914 – writes: 'Shall I still be love's house on the *widdershin* earth, / Woe to the windy mansions at my shelter?' Usually in its plural form, the creepy adjective *widdershins* means 'luckless', 'accursed', or 'related to occult practices'. It derives from Germanic roots meaning 'the wrong way' or 'in a hostile way', and can mean this as an adverb too in English. Traditionally, a suspected vampire is turned *widdershins* in the grave (buried face-down) in order to prevent escape.

There are many other wrong ways for things to turn – if one's hair stands *widdershins* it is on end, because one has received a fright – but the primary one historically was to go in the opposite direction from the sun's apparent movement, and so anticlockwise (not *deisal*: see 21 February). To do so has anciently been considered an invitation to catastrophe at best, or a deliberate invocation of evil spirits at worst. In 1685, the mathematician and engineeer George Sinclair published his rather sensationally titled *Satan's Invisible World Discovered*, a collection of purportedly authentic accounts of witchcraft, in which a 'witch dance' is described thus: 'The men turned nine times *Widder-shines* about, and the Women six times.' Don't try it at home.

28 October

Ectype

The word *ectype* comes from the Greek for 'out' and 'figure', meaning 'something worked in relief'. In English it has been used in this literal sense to mean a wax impression of a seal; but more often it means a copy, and often with some of the same negative associations. Thomas Blount says *ectype* means 'a thing made according to the example and copy; a counterfeit', so a forgery, while other writers use it to mean something that was later run off from the original, so the opposite of the *prototype* (literally, 'first figure') or *archetype* ('high figure'). Such reproductions, it is often implied, are subject to error and degradation.

The philosopher John Locke, who died on this day in 1704, argued that because our ideas of external substances are formed from combining our simple sense-impressions of their various qualities (colour, shape, touch, and so forth), the resulting complex ideas cannot be expected to represent the substances themselves accurately and in full. Thus: 'The complex ideas of substances are *ectypes*, copies too; but not perfect ones, not adequate.' In today's era of rampant and iterated copycat art and outright plagiarism, meanwhile, we could do worse than denounce the resurgence of *ectype* culture.

Gulosity

An insatiably greedy person is one given to *gulosity*, a sonorous and somehow stomach-stretching word (from the Latin for 'gullet') to be employed when *gluttony* simply doesn't go far enough. James Boswell, the Scottish writer and biographer of Samuel Johnson, who was born on this day in 1740, remarks that his friend's disquisition in Issue 206 of *The Rambler* is 'a masterly essay against *gulosity*'.

Indeed it is: in 'The Art of Living at the Cost of Others', Dr Johnson invents a pointedly named character, *Gulosulus*, a mediocre parasite who haunts other people's dinners. 'His chief policy,' Johnson writes, 'consists in selecting some dish from every course, and recommending it to the company, with an air so decisive, that no one ventures to contradict him. By this practice he acquires at a feast a kind of dictatorial authority; his taste becomes the standard of pickles and seasoning, and he is venerated by the professors of epicurism, as the only man who understands the niceties of cookery ... By this method of life Gulosulus has so impressed on his imagination the dignity of feasting, that he has no other topic of talk, or subject of meditation.' Our modern pandemic of *gulosity*, it seems, is not so new after all.

Periplum

The poet Ezra Pound was born on this day in 1885, and among other things has left to us the word *periplum*. Entire scholarly books have been devoted to explicating this concept, but essentially it signifies the subjective experience of a voyage, particularly a roundabout one. It derives from the classical term for an account of a circumnavigation (Latin *periplus*, Greek *periplous*), and at one point Pound uses it to mean: 'not as land looks on a map / But as sea bord seen by men sailing'.

Periplum is also related by Pound to Odysseus's epic journey, and to 'the cool of the 42nd St. tunnel' (in New York City). A story of a man who stole a safe he couldn't open, Pound remarks, could be entitled 'periplum by camion [truck]'. Old Ezra would surely be pleased if we decided to make our shopping trip or commute seem more exotic by setting off on a *periplum*.

31 October

Circumforaneous

This being Hallowe'en, you might encounter many *circumforaneous* persons. From the Latin *circum*, 'around', and *forum*, 'market', from 1650 it meant literally 'wandering from market to market', and so 'vagrant' or 'vagabond'. But then markets became specifically houses, and to be *circumforaneous* was to go from home to home in search of favours – perhaps in exchange for some entertainment. A troupe of actors might engage in '*circumforaneous* Masking or Mumming' (1664), while Dr Johnson noted the phenomenon of 'A *circumforaneous* fiddler', who was 'one that plays at doors'. In contrast to which horrors, a bit of juvenile trick-or-treating might not sound so bad after all.

November

1 November

Mooncalf

In Shakespeare's *The Tempest* – performed at court on this day, All Hallows, in 1611 – the butler Stephano offers some wine to Prospero's slave, Caliban, and then asks: 'How now, *mooncalf*, how does thine ague?' A *mooncalf*, as the word suggests, was an unnatural creation, a monster, and sometimes an actual calf that lived on the moon, as encountered by the astronauts centuries later in H. G. Wells's *The First Men in the Moon* (1901).

But in the interim the word's usage had softened, so that it was most often used to mean a daydreamer or simpleton. In Dickens's *Barnaby Rudge* (1841), Gabriel reproaches himself for not questioning a woman more severely, 'instead of standing gaping at her, like an old mooncalf as I am!' So to this day a *mooncalf* can be an absent-minded or sentimental person, as well as the kind of idea or project that might occur to such a fellow. Once one has the word, one may find that there are *mooncalves* everywhere one looks.

Cunctation

The English poet Robert Herrick achieved renown in his lifetime for his collected works, published as *Hesperides* in 1648, which contains the famous line 'Gather ye rosebuds while ye may', as well as an astonishing total of 1,400 poems. Some of them, it is true, are very short, such as a two-liner entitled 'Delay', which reads, in proper *carpe diem* fashion: 'Break off delay, since we but read of one / That ever prospered by *cunctation*.'

Cunctation is delaying or deferral, perhaps with some cunning in mind (Latin *cunctari*, 'to delay'). The one who prospered by *cunctation* did so quite deliberately: the Roman commander Quintus Fabius Maximus Verrucosus became celebrated for his clever delaying tactics against Hannibal, and was therefore nicknamed *Cunctator*. In military thinking, this subsequently became known as 'Fabian strategy', and inspired in turn the name of the Fabian Society in late nineteenth-century Britain, which aimed to introduce socialism not through sudden revolution but through gradual erosion of resistance. Its most prominent pamphleteer was the Irish playwright George Bernard Shaw, who died on this day in 1950.

Atrate

One who, like Prince Hamlet, dresses all in inky shades is an *atrate*, as Cockeram's 1623 *Dictionary* has it: 'One clad in black, a mourner.' From the Latin *ater* ('black'), *atrate* also appears as the name of the black vulture (*Coragyps atratus*), and as an old botanical term for the blackening of vegetable tissue.

In modern times, of course, one doesn't need to be in mourning to be an *atrate*, and such stylish persons may be seen everywhere. Let us dedicate the word, then, to the Man in Black himself, Johnny Cash, whose second studio album, *The Fabulous Johnny Cash*, was released on this day in 1958.

Luciferous

Something that is *luciferous* brings light, as the angel Lucifer (Latin for 'light-bearer') himself once did, before being cast down. A torch or lamp, the Sun itself, or animals that glow in the dark, may all be described as *luciferous*, but so might a book or argument, with a parallel metaphoric sense to that of *enlightening*. (This sense was inspired by Francis Bacon's maxim '*Lucifera experimenta, non fructifera quaerenda*': *luciferous* experiments are those that do not multiply questions.)

So the term was used by the theologican and philosopher Joseph Glanvill, who died on this day in 1680. In his modestly titled *Essays on Several Important Subjects in Philosophy and Religion* (1676), he refers to the scientist Robert Boyle's airpump experiments, which have proved 'a rare and *luciferous Theory, viz.* the *Elastick Power* or *Spring* of the *Air*'.

5 NOVEMBER

Chumping

In England this is Bonfire Night, when the attempt to blow up the Houses of Parliament by the anarchist Guy Fawkes is celebrated with the decorative blowing-up of innumerable small explosives, in the form of fireworks, and an enormous fire on which Fawkes is burned in effigy, even though he was actually sentenced to be hanged, drawn, and quartered (and, to his good fortune, died at the first).

For such a big fire you need a lot of wood, and *chumping* is the method by which you collect it. A *chump* itself is a short, thick piece of wood (and so, metaphorically, a stupid person), so people in the nineteenth century would make a festival out of several days' worth of *chumping* in preparation for this evening's pyromaniac celebrations. Modern urbanists have less need to collect wood, but *chumping* could as well be used for the collection of anything else considered desirable for the evening's entertainment, including sparklers, warm gloves, and perhaps a hip flask.

Singult

If one is in poetic distress, one might emit a *singult*, which means a sob. It derives from the Latin *singultus* ('sob' or any 'sharp catching of breath') which is now used as the medical term for a hiccup.

The poet William Browne, whose example inspired the young Milton, and whose estate formally passed to his widow on this day in 1645, uses the term in his *Britannia's Pastorals* (1616), where we witness a young woman crying inconsolably in a wood, in a description that is rather unsentimentally graphic: 'So when her tears were stopp'd from either eye, / Her *singults*, blubb'rings, seem'd to make them fly / Out at her oyster-mouth and nostrils wide.' As you might imagine, in Elizabethan poetry *singults* were usually heard from women; happily, in later literature men could experience them too.

Querimonious

If you know someone who is always complaining, you can give them something else to complain about by calling them *querimonious*. It comes from the Latin *queri*, 'to complain' – from where we also get *query*, which in its earliest English uses also implied a note of complaint or objection rather than a neutral question. *Querimonious* itself is first recorded in Robert Cawdrey's *A Table Alphabeticall*, one of the earliest English dictionaries, in 1604, and the never-satisfied have been called it ever since. A picturesque example of the use is that by a naturalist writing in the *Journal of Mammology* in 1999 that the build-up of a badger's snarl was *querimonious*. Such badgers are not to be messed with.

The best way to deal with *querimonious* persons might be to encourage them to recognize and embrace the cruelty and meaningless of the universe, and so to refrain from grousing and whining about the inescapable absurdity of existence. Such was the recipe for happiness offered by the French writer Albert Camus, who was born on this day in 1913.

Abluvion

Don't, as the saying has it, flush the infant down with the *abluvion*, the latter being a usefully precise word for bathwater and all it contains, or any other effluent that goes down the drain. It is first recorded in the second edition of *Letters of the British Spy* (1805) by William Wirt, who was born on this day in 1772, and was not in fact a British spy but a lawyer who later became the longest-serving US Attorney General. In his book, written in the character of a young British nobleman who travels through America, Wirt discusses the theory of the time that the Earth's rotation causes the eastern coasts of continents to grow by accretion of material. One expert, he says, 'in the constant *abluvion* from the western coast of one continent, has found a perennial source of materials for the eastern coast of that which lies behind it'.

From the Latin *abluere*, to wash off or wash away, *abluvion* is the kind of stuff that, with modern plumbing, one happily consigns to oblivion, until fatbergs appear in the sewers.

Catachrestical

The English writer George Puttenham was celebrated for his book of literary history and poetic criticism *The Arte of English Poesie*, which was entered in the Stationers' Register on this day in 1588. It contains the first recorded reference in English to '*Catachresis*, or the Figure of abuse'. From the Greek for 'misuse', this is the practice of abusing some name or phrase by employing it in a sense other than its correct one. So the clergyman and poet John Reynolds complained that the planets were given '*Catachrestical* names', because Mars was dark and cold, so 'how can he bear / The name of the Old Pagan God of War?'

Coleridge subsequently devoted paragraphs to rebutting the common proverb that 'fortune favours fools'. On the one hand, he pointed out, the envious might call fools people who are simply brave; and on the other hand, wise men might successfully aim at what the common world does not call fortune. 'In this sense,' Coleridge concluded, 'the proverb is current by a misuse, or a *catachresis* at least, of both the words, fortune and fools.' The word is still of use in a world where so much argument is *catachrestical*.

10 NOVEMBER

Caliginous

Dark, gloomy, dim, obscure . . . when one wants to emphasize a poverty of light, it is easy to run out of synonyms. We might therefore resurrect the beautiful adjective *caliginous*, from the Latin for 'misty'. Cowper's translation of the *Odyssey*, for example, boasts the line: 'The goddess enter'd deep the cave *Caliginous*.' The word is also casually employed by Dr Johnson's friend Hester Lynch Piozzi (formerly Thrale) in her 1794 usage guide, *British Synonymy*, where she writes of 'That *caliginous* atmosphere which fills London towards the 10th of November'. In London one doesn't necessarily have to wait till so near the end of the year to experience a *caliginous* ambience, but in honour of Piozzi let us nonetheless celebrate the word today.

Eleventy

On the eleventh day of the eleventh month, what better word to celebrate than *eleventy*, meaning 'some vaguely large number'? It is of pleasingly antique vintage, first recorded by the *OED* in 1841 – 'We calculate about eleven hundred and eleventy-eleven [carriages]' – and has proven irresistible ever since. One might at first wonder why the anonymous coiner skipped straight from ninety to *eleventy*, until one learns that *tenty* means something else (see 1 August).

Serious folk who protest that *eleventy* is just a made-up number should know that it received the imprimatur of no less a writer than J. R. R. Tolkien. In *The Fellowship of the Ring* (1954), we read: 'Mr Bilbo Baggins of Bag End announced that he would shortly be celebrating his eleventy-first birthday.' By that time, of course, the hero of *The Hobbit* was really rather old.

Benedicence

This is a rare word for what might seem itself to be in the process of becoming rarer: kindness of speech. It was coined by the nineteenth-century Sanskritologist, born on this day in 1819, who gloried in the name Sir Monier Monier-Williams, this not being due to an oversight on the part of his parents but his own peculiar taste for nominative *epizeuxis* (see 30 November), for he was born plain old Monier Williams, and only later decided to add his first name to his surname as well.

Writing of the tenets of the Zoroastrian faith, Monier-Williams says that a follower 'was to be rewarded hereafter not according to his belief in any particular religious dogma, but according to the perfection of his thoughts, words, and deeds; of his benevolence, his *benedicence* (if I may coin a new word), and his beneficence'. Why yes, Sir Monier, you may. From the Latin for 'well-speaking' (just as *benevolence* means 'well-wishing' and *beneficence* 'well-doing'), *benedicence* is still occasionally used in religious circles to mean 'charity in speech', but it surely deserves wider currency, as naming a thing might encourage its uptake.

13 November

Refulgent

What is *refulgent* is gleaming, shining, or radiant, directly from the Latin verb *refulgere*, and has a particular sense of splendour. So, the blonde hair of one poet's beloved was *refulgent*, and so was the steel armour of another's mighty hero.

Robert Louis Stevenson was born on this day in 1850. In his travel memoir *In the South Seas* (1896), he writes of his company aboard a ship at night struggling to make out the Polynesian island, Takaroa, they were supposed to be arriving at: 'By and by not only islands, but *refulgent* and revolving lights began to stud the darkness; lighthouses of the mind or of the wearied optic nerve, solemnly shining and winking as we passed.' (Spoiler: they were lost, and landed at another atoll thirty miles distant the next morning.) 'Lighthouses of the mind' seems too good a phrase not to adopt metaphorically for all kinds of misleading notions: it is itself a *refulgent* phrase.

Psittacism

The great mathematician and scientist Gottfried Wilhelm Leibniz, who died on this day in 1716, has too many accomplishments to list here, among them the independent discovery (along with Newton) of the calculus, but he also introduced a very useful new word to the lexicon: *psitta-cism*. This is the English version of Leibniz's Latin coinage *Psittazismus*, and comes from the Greek for 'parrot'. Thus, just as we say that one may *parrot* received ideas, *psittacism* is the act of parroting, particularly of repeating impressive-sounding formulations without really understanding what they mean.

The term was introduced (rather unsuccessfully, it must be admitted) to literary criticism by I. A. Richards and C. K. Ogden in *The Meaning of Meaning* (1923) – *psittacism*, they said, was 'the use of words without reference' – but it would surely merit wider application. One academic in the 1990s, for instance, admitted sorrowfully that there was a kind of 'scholarly *psittacism*' afoot, and it might even be perceived outside the academy walls to this day.

15 November

Calque

Today being the dubiously named I Love To Write Day, let us honour a peculiarly literary term. When one language borrows a phrase from another by translating it literally word for word, it is a *calque*. The word *calque* itself is first recorded in the journal of the American Dialect Society in 1937: it comes from the French *calquer*, to copy or trace (e.g., an outline), which in turn derives from the Latin *calcare*, to tread.

When you start looking for them, indeed, *calques* are everywhere. For example, the French *marché aux puces* (a market with fleas in it) was adopted into English as the *calque* 'flea-market', while the English word *brainwashing* is a *calque* from the Chinese *xǐ nǎo*, adopted by the US military in Korea, and *assault rifle* is a *calque* from the German *Sturmgewehr*, a rifle in use towards the end of the Second World War. Pleasingly, the more common term for *calque*, 'loan-word', comes from the German *Lehnwort*, and so is itself a *calque*.

Dungeonable

A *dungeonable* fellow is one fit to be confined to a dungeon: a malicious or diabolical person. It is first recorded in 1691 in a glossary of northern English dialect: 'A Dungeonable Body; a shrewd person, or, as the vulgar express it, a divellish Fellow.' (*Shrewd* once meant 'depraved' or 'wicked', before passing into a weaker sense of 'clever'.)

In mid-nineteenth-century Yorkshire, however, it was also possible to use *dungeonable* to mean 'extremely knowledge-able' ('deep' in the sense of 'knowing'). This seems more respectfully fitting to describe aficionados of the role-playing game Dungeons & Dragons, or those who happily haunt the dungeons of the Zelda videogames designed by Shigeru Miyamoto, who was born on this day in 1952. The original sense, however, seems to have the potential for wider use among the general population. Whom do you consider fit to be thrown in a dungeon?

Mawworm

The Irish playwright Isaac Bickerstaff saw his satire *The Hypocrite*, an adaptation of Molière's *Tartuffe*, premiere on this night in 1768. Bickerstaff's original contribution to the story is a character called 'Mr. *Maw-worm*', a religious enthusiast who refuses to believe the evidence of his own eyes. Since the sixteenth century, *maw-worm* had been the name for a parasitic stomach-worm (*maw*, 'stomach'), of the genus later identified as *Ascaris*, that afflicts humans and other mammals. After the success of Bickerstaff's play, however, *mawworm* became a popular term for someone who was an excessively pious-seeming but hypocritical person.

It is used thus by George Eliot in *Middlemarch* (1872), when Sir James thinks to himself 'that he had chosen the one who was in all respects the superior; and a man naturally likes to look forward to having the best. He would be the very *Mawworm* of bachelors who pretended not to expect it.' The *OED* tells us that the word *mawworm* is 'now rare', though the type of human being it describes, regrettably, is not.

Objurgate

To *objurgate* someone is to scold them severely (straight-forwardly from the Latin *obiurgare*, 'to rebuke'). You can, as people have, *objurgate* your enemies, a rowing team-mate who has missed his stroke, or a horse. To *objurgate* can also be, simply, to moan, to complain, or to rail against something.

The vorticist painter and writer Wyndham Lewis was born on this day in 1882; in his critique of (among other things) consumer capitalism, *The Art of Being Ruled* (1926), he writes, of Friedrich Nietzsche: 'He provided a sanction and licence ... for LIFE – the very life that he never ceased himself to *objurgate* against; the life of the second-rate and shoddily emotional, for the person, very unfortunately, smart and rich enough to be able to regard himself as an "aristo-crat", a man "beyond good and evil", a destroying angel and cultivated Mephistopheles.' This is a bit unfair on Nietzsche, but it is rather a thrilling example of rhetorical *objurgation*.

19 November

Rantipole

A person who is *rantipole* is one who is 'wild; roving; rakish', says Dr Johnson, adding disapprovingly: 'A low word.' Low it might be, but it is fun to say if one needs an alternative term for 'roguish' or 'vagabondish'. Already by the late seventeenth century the word was well-enough known that it could be used as a character's indicative surname in satire. The 1679 comedy *A True Widow*, by Thomas Shadwell – who died on this day in 1692 – contains reference to a certain Sir Thomas Rantipol, reported as having lost six hundred pounds in a night's gambling, an impressive sum in those days.

Authorities think *rantipole* is probably formed from *rant*, as in 'wild speaking', and *pole* or *poll*, meaning 'head'. As a term of abuse it gradually acquired the extra sense of 'irrational' or 'mad', as well as 'wild' and 'boisterous'. A writer for the London *Times* was perhaps intending all the above meanings when he observed in 1841: 'Nor can it provoke the slightest astonishment that these *rantipole* politicians should treat any promise with scorn, and pursue any object which flatters their vanity with extreme recklessness.' An evergreen phenomenon.

Scripturiency

Scripturiency is a passion for writing – or at least an unignorable urge to write, whether one enjoys doing so or not. Unhappily, in its earliest use the word meant an urge to write masses of rubbish: *scripturiency*, wrote one seventeenth-century commentator, was 'a fault in feeble pens'; another referred to 'the Disease of *Scripturiency*'. On this day in 1717, Issue 3 of the weekly magazine *The Entertainer* (*Containing Remarks Upon Men, Manners, Religion, Policy, etc.*) referred wittily to a 'bladder of *scripturiency*', and we may imagine that what issues from a bladder will hardly be worth *scrutation* (see 17 September).

Still, what is a fault in feeble pens may yet be a virtue in strong ones. In any case, no one has yet found a cure for the syndrome, and it remains true that, as the book of Ecclesiastes has it, 'Of making many books there is no end.'

21 November

Doryphore

A pedantic quibbler, forever chasing after the minor faults of others, is a *doryphore*. The word comes from the French name for the potato-eating Colorado beetle, which in turn comes from the Greek for 'spear-carrier'. It was Englished in this sense by the British politician and writer Harold Nicolson, born on this day in 1886, who in an article of 1949 complained about nitpicking critics thus: 'These Colorado beetles will spent hours searching for a misprint in the *Oxford English Dictionary* ... Although these doryphores may achieve the short delight of proving that an author has made a mistake on page 479, they will never know the slow, long pleasure of writing a large book with continuous application.'

Should any helpful *doryphores* wish to draw the author's attention to errors in the present book, they will of course not be so insulted.

Infundibuliform

Some words are to be recommended simply because they are fun to look at and fun to say: so, should you ever wish to describe something as funnel-shaped, you should seize the opportunity to use the adjective *infundibuliform*, which derives from the Latin for 'an instrument for pouring in'.

The physician and actor Sir John Hill, who died on this day in 1775, wrote in his *A History of Animals* (1752) of the lumpfish: 'The ventral fins coalesce at their extremities, and form a single, oblong hollow, and, in some degree, *infundibuliform* fin.' Perhaps this was not guaranteed to form a clear picture in the reader's mind, but later descriptions of *infundibuliform* flowers do have a graphic prettiness. To this day, one sometimes requires an *infundibuliform* utensil in the kitchen, and to say so will mark one out as quite the culinary expert.

Acronical

Thomas Henderson, the Scottish astronomer who was the first person to measure the distance to Alpha Centauri, died on this day in 1844; it is his discipline that gives rise to the word *acronical*. From the Greek *acro*– ('relating to height') and *nux* ('night'), *acronical* (or *acronic*) denotes the rising or setting of a celestial body that occurs around sunset. Such astronomical terms have often proved irresistible for declarations of erotic bedazzlement, and so the Scottish writer Sir Thomas Urquhart describes in his *The Jewel* (1652) a certain young lady whose 'appearance was like the antartick oriency of a western aurora, or *acronick* rising of the most radiant constellation of the firmament'.

In 1930 an American science writer borrowed the word to mean simply 'at sunset', declaring: 'An *acronical* view over the Grand Canyon is worth more than the Apollo of Praxiteles.' Perhaps, but the word might still be of most use to amorous literary types.

Videnda

What modern travel guides call the 'sights' of a destination
– rather stupidly, since literally everything the visitor lays
eyes on will be a *sight*, regardless of its cultural interest or
antiquity – used to be called, more accurately, the *videnda*.
This being a Latin gerund (like *agenda* or – see 4 December
– *tacenda*), it means 'the things that ought to be seen'. So
one eighteenth-century correspondent enthused, of a travel
guide, that it contained 'the *Videnda* in all parts of Great
Britain, as Houses, Antiquities, Views, &c.', while another,
more disappointed traveller complained of being 'humbug'd
by printed accounts of visionary *Videnda*'.

The term is first recorded, though, in *The Life and
Opinions of Tristram Shandy* (1759–67), the success of which
presumably popularized it. Here, the hero explains his inten-
tion to see the 'tomb of the lovers': 'In my list, therefore, of
Videnda at Lyons, this, though *last* – was not, you see, *least*.'
Tristram's author, the incomparable Laurence Sterne, was
born on this day in 1713.

Fallalery

Cheap-looking finery and tawdry accessorizing of the kind that not we but other people indulge in may be called *fallalery*, a word the OED suggests might be related to the French *falbala*, 'an ornamental frill', and also to *falderal*, 'a trifle', and *fa-la-la*, imitative of superficial singing. Happily, if we are not so interested in criticizing others' dress sense, we may still employ *fallalery* in disapproval of what we consider silly or trifling behaviour, while abandoning the old prejudice that such comportment was the exclusive preserve of women.

In 1977, a theatre reviewer for the *Spectator* referred to 'female fallalery', as though it were a well-established phenomenon, while at the same time complimenting the playwright who had attributed such *fallalery* 'not to innate psychology, but to the social and economic system of patriarchy'. Let us charitably say, perhaps, that he got halfway there. The play in question was the 1910 domestic satire *The Madras House*, by Harley Granville-Barker, who was born on this day in 1877.

Delator

A *delator* is 'he that secretly accuseth' (Thomas Blount), an informer or secret snitch. The first recorded use of the word (from the Latin for 'report' or 'accuse'), however, warns against the obvious problem that *delators* might have ulterior motives. In his *History of the Reformation of Scotland* (1572), John Knox writes of a time when 'Whosoever would *delate* any of heresy, he was heard: no respect nor consideration had what mind the *delator* bore to the person *delated*.' Indeed, a later Scottish historian, John Spottiswoode, who died on this day in 1639, writes of one bishop who enjoyed good relations with the French king, until, 'as it falleth out often in courts, upon some envious *delations*, the king became jealous of him, as if he had practised with some noblemen against the royal succession'.

Delator is too good a word, however, to save for stories of court politicking: it is the perfect term, for example, to describe those who, in our time, report material they claim to be offensive to online moderators, in hopes of getting their enemies silenced.

Fetor

What's that smell? If it is a particularly offensive odour, you may signal lordly disgust by calling it a *fetor*. This is the splendid noun form of the more common adjective *fetid* (or *foetid*), both deriving from the Latin *fetere*, 'to stink'. It is one of the pungently obscure terms employed by the American writer James Agee, who was born on this day in 1909. In his celebrated account of poor American farmers during the Great Depression, *Let Us Now Praise Famous Men* (1941), he evokes the aromas of 'pork, lard, corn, woodsmoke, pine, and ammonia' in their homes, and expands: 'I should further describe the odor of corn: in sweat, or on the teeth, and breath, when it is eaten as much as they eat it, it is of a particularly sweet stuffy *fetor*, to which the nearest parallel is the odor of the yellow excrement of a baby.'

The first recorded use of *fetor* is the cheering observation, in the medieval *Mirror of Man's Salvation* (c. 1429), that 'this wily world' will in the end fill a man 'with rottenness and *fetor*'. On a brighter note, the Arctic explorer Elisha Kent Kane explained in 1856 that she preferred the meat of a female seal, because it 'has not the *fetor* of her mate's', and was tastier than reindeer. Even in our deodorized age, one often still has the choice only between two *fetors*.

Coarctate

This day in 1660 saw the inaugural meeting of the Royal Society, the world's oldest scientific academy. Among those present was the chemist Robert Boyle, who later wrote in an account of one of his innumerable experiments: 'Air is contained in Bread, but it is so closely *coarctated* therein, that no easy operation can give it a discharge.' To *coarctate* (from the Latin for 'to press together' or 'to compel') is to compress or squeeze close together, or to confine within strict limits. Thomas Blount, for his part, says it is also used for the tightening up of prose: '*Coarctate*, to strain, to gather a matter into few words, to shorten.' One might wish that more books had been properly *coarctated*.

Gove

To *gove* is to goggle mindlessly, to gawp, or gape, or, as the old expression has it, 'to stare like a stuck pig'. In his winningly titled dictionary *A Collection of English Words Not Generally Used* (1674), the English naturalist and theologian John Ray, who was born on this day in 1627, says that the word is used of 'persons that unhandsomely gaze or look about them'. Later writers would use *gove* to imply a sort of bestial dullness, including in beasts themselves: the Scottish poet James Hogg, in his poem 'Bonny Kilmeny', writes that when his heroine sang prettily in the woods: 'The wild beasts of the forests came ... / And *goved* around, charmed and amazed; / Even the dull cattle crooned and gazed.' This helpful word is now confined by lexicologists to the category of Scottish and Northern English dialect, which is a shame, because it's not as though there aren't just as many *govers* the world over as there used to be.

Epizeuxis

Winston Churchill, who was born on this day in 1874, was perhaps the greatest rhetorician in English of the twentieth century. Among the devices he employed with mastery is the figure of *epizeuxis*, which comes from the Greek for 'fastening together', and means the repetition of a word or phrase several times in short succession, to create a feeling of vehemence or insistence. A celebrated example of *epizeuxis* is a speech Churchill gave in October 1941: 'This is the lesson: never give in, never give in, never, never, never – in nothing, great or small, large or petty – *never give in*, except to convictions of honour and good sense. Never yield to force; never yield to the apparently overwhelming might of the enemy.'

An *epizeuxis* on the same word, but in tragic mode, occurs when King Lear realizes that his youngest daughter Cordelia is dead. 'Oh, thou'lt come no more, / Never, never, never, never, never.'

December

1 December

Sprucify

It is a shame to write that you aim to 'spruce up' something when there is the pretty word *sprucify* lying around neglected. To *sprucify* has meant to neaten or decorate – or, if you will, to pimp up – since the early seventeenth century. This is because, in the fourteenth and fifteenth centuries, *Spruce* was another name for Prussia, whence luxury goods were often imported, such as *spruce leather* and *spruce ochre* dye. The *spruce tree*, in turn, was so named because this source of excellent wood was believed to be native to Prussia as well.

In Victorian times, Christmas trees were put up on the afternoon of Christmas Eve, but these days it is more common, and more festive, to have them around for the whole month. In Britain, the most common species for this application is the Norway spruce, so in decorating it today you can happily say that you are *sprucifying* your spruce.

2 December

Nugacity

If the futility of existence is wearing, you might be cheered up by knowing that there is a very pretty alternative word for 'futility', viz. *nugacity*. From the Latin *nugax* ('insignificant'), *nugacity* originally meant a trifling or frivolous thing, and the sense of triviality then spilled over into the gloomy feeling that absolutely everything is trivial.

As Philip Larkin, who died on this day in 1985, wrote to Kingsley Amis six years previously: 'I'm sorry this letter is so dull, but I do just bugger all and tend to stagnate. One gets obsessed with *nugacity* (you are bound to know what that means, you sod).' No doubt he did. And don't we all?

3 December

Litotes

Someone who habitually employs *litotes* (pronounced lighTOATees) is likely to say, when absolutely *furibund* (see 21 December), that he is not a little irked; or, when famished, that he is not unpeckish. Straight from the Greek for 'smoothness', 'plainness', or 'smallness', it is a rhetorical device in which you say something by negating its opposite: 'It was no small affair', 'She is not unattractive', and so forth. The word first appears in print in 1656 in *The Mysterie of Rhetorique Unveil'd*, probably by the theologian John Sergeant. Among writers fond of *litotes* was Robert Louis Stevenson, who died on this day in 1894: 'It was *not unpleasant*, in such an humour, to catch sight, ever and anon, of large spaces of the open plain . . .'

More loosely, *litotes* can mean any kind of ironical under-statement, which is how it seems to be employed in the majestic literary satire *Peri Bathous: Or, the Art of Sinking*, usually attributed to Alexander Pope (1727). Therein, the reader is given a handy list of the common rhetorical tricks indulged in by people from all walks of society, from politicians and courtiers to fishmongers and bear-baiters. But *litotes*, or 'diminution', we are told, is the 'peculiar talent' of 'ladies, whisperers, and backbiters'.

Tacenda

If you are tired of having an agenda, you might decide instead to concentrate on your *tacenda*. 'Agenda' is the Latin neutral plural gerund from *agere*, to do, and so means 'things to be done'; similarly, *tacenda* is formed from the Latin *tacere*, to remain silent, and so means 'things not to be mentioned'. The Scottish historian Thomas Carlyle, born on this day in 1795, is the first writer recorded by the *OED* as using it, writing in *Past and Present* (1843) about the monkish habit of gossiping: 'How one hooded head applies itself to the ear of another, and whispers – *tacenda*.'

Ludwig Wittgenstein's *Tractatus Logico-Philosophicus* (1922) famously ends with proposition 7: 'Whereof one cannot speak, thereof one must be silent.' Modern society might be improved if more things were thus designated *tacenda*.

5 December

Blatherskite

There being so much nonsense talked in the modern age, we still arguably have need of the splenetic word *blatherskite*, which can mean either 'idiotic speech', or a person given to emitting it. Originally, *bletherskate* was a Scottish formation from *blether* (to ramble on nonsensically) and *skate* in the sense of a worn-out horse. American soldiers during the War of Independence had among their favourite camp songs a Scottish ditty called 'Maggie Lauder', which contains the line 'Jog on your gait, ye *bletherskate*' (sometimes written *bladder-skate*), and so it passed into American slang for a senseless blusterer or his wearying emanations.

Not just American, though: the English existentialist writer Colin Wilson, who died on this day in 2013, wrote in his most famous book, *The Outsider* (1956), that 'For Nietzsche ... there is no such thing as abstract knowledge; there is only useful knowledge and unprofitable *blatherskite*.' You might suspect there is now more of the latter than ever before.

Floccify

To *floccify* something is to think it worthless, to set nothing by it. It comes from the Latin *flocci facere*, a favourite formulation of Cicero's, that literally means 'to value something as much as a small wisp of wool'. That is also part of the derivation of the comically amplified coinage *floccinaucinihilipilification*, which comes from the series of Latin words conveying a sense of little worth (*flocci, nauci, nihili, pili*), and was introduced in a letter by the poet, essayist and landscape gardener William Shenstone, who was baptized on this day in 1714.

Floccify itself is not quite confined to the dictionaries, for a few nineteenth-century writers essayed it in the literary magazines, and it still lacks a close single-word equivalent in English. 'Who expects eutrapely [courtesy] in the House of Commons?' one correspondent asked in 1890. 'All its members *floccify* [think little of] each other.' Their opinions do not seem to have improved much since.

Balter

As one might be observed doing at a party around this time of year, to *balter* is to dance clumsily or otherwise tumble about. (It comes, probably, from the Old Norse for the same thing.) In a sixteenth-century Scottish song of rustic partying, it is observed that 'sum trottit' (danced well), while 'sum *balterit*' (careered around). Usefully, *balter* can also mean to mat or knot the hair, or to clog with something sticky. In honour of all these meanings, there is now an annual Balter Festival in England where one can enjoy silly dancing and a lack of cleanliness.

W. H. Auden uses the word figuratively in his poem 'Under Sirius': 'Yes, these are the dog days, Fortunatus: / The heather lies limp and dead / On the mountain, the *baltering* torrent / Shrunk to a soodling thread.' One unfortunate reviewer of the collection, whom it is kinder not to name, complained that it was full of 'nonce-words' like *baltering*, imagining that it meant something that was once *battering* but was now *faltering*. Some marks, we might agree, for creativity, but none for not consulting the dictionary.

Sciolist

A *sciolist* is someone of that familiar type who is desperate to have it thought that he possesses more learning than he really does. From the Latin *sciolus*, 'a pretender to knowledge', it would thus seem a rather topical word for an age of hastily researched *philippics* (see 10 June) and pseudotechnical conspiracy theories.

On this day in 1752 was born the splendidly named Vicesimus Knox, a writer, teacher, and popular theorist of sensibility and good conduct, who in an autobiographical essay recounts sternly the frivolities of his youth: 'By constant frequenting the playhouses, and mixing with contemptible *sciolists*, who called themselves theatrical critics, I became … enamoured of the stage.' No good, of course, could come of that.

9 DECEMBER

Pandemonium

This word is today generally used to mean any kind of chaos, omnishambles, or clusterfuck, but its original meaning is more infernally specific. Born on this day in 1608, the poet John Milton coined *pandæmonium* from the Greek *pan*– (meaning 'all') and *daimon* (meaning 'demon'), and then, not worried about mixing his Classical languages, added the Latin suffix *–ium*, as found in many abstract nouns (e.g. *odium*, *tedium*) and also Roman place names, such as Londinium.

In *Paradise Lost* (1667), *Pandæmonium*, like Londinium, is a city – but a city of devils. It is 'the high Capital / Of Satan and his Peers', or later the 'City and proud seat / Of Lucifer' – Lucifer, or 'bearer of light' (see 4 November), being Satan's original name before he was cast out of heaven. *Pandemonium* was briefly also used as a synonym for the 'tailor's hell', the place under the shop counter where the tailor would keep odd scraps and offcuts of material — or even, according to some aggrieved commentators, bits stolen while measuring out a customer's yards. Cheeringly its modern application is much more versatile, able to denote all manner of frightful mess or delightful revelry.

Preceptor

A *preceptor* (from Latin *praeceptor*) was once an expert in writing, and then more generally a tutor or instructor, though he could for a while also have been the leader of a local chapter (or *preceptory*) of the Knights Templar or Hospitallers. Since then the word has been especially valued among poets to describe an exemplary 'master' who formed the speaker's own practice: both Emily Dickinson – born on this day in 1830 – and, later, Philip Larkin used the word in this way; and a *preceptor* has also been used to denote a person who trains doctors.

With such an artistic, scientific, and swashbuckling history, perhaps *preceptor* should be used more often to encourage an attitude of deeper respect towards teachers of all kinds.

Phylactery

A *phylactery*, from the Greek for 'amulet', originally specified a leather box containing Torah texts, worn by Jewish men during prayer, but then came to mean any kind of religious observance. Since the seventeenth century, the *OED* notes, its use in this general sense has been 'frequently depreciative', coming to mean something like an unexamined prejudice. Against the modern reverence for honesty at all times, for example, one may lay this remark in a sermon from 1796: 'Candour is the grand *Phylactery* of every perturbed spirit – and oftentimes means nothing more than inchoate Rebellion.' The preacher was Henry William Coulthurst, who was born into a slave-owning family in Barbados, but then became an ardent abolitionist, and who died on this day in 1817.

Phylactery might also prove a useful word in politics. The Earl of Rosebery, writer, politician (and, briefly, prime minister in 1894–5), later wrote: 'There are men who sit still with the fly-blown *phylacteries* of obsolete policies bound round their foreheads, who do not remember that, while they have been mumbling their incantations to themselves, the world has been marching and revolving.' There are such people still.

12 December

Borborygm

Sensibly, the Greeks had a dedicated verb, probably onomatopoeic in origin, for having a rumbling in the bowels, which found its way into English in the form of *borborygm*, or the Latinate *borborgymus*. The physician and scientist Erasmus Darwin, grandfather of Charles, was born on this day in 1731, and employs the word naturally in his seminal 1794 work *Zoonomia, or, the Laws of Organic Life*: 'The hysteric disease is attended with inverted motions feebly exerted of the œsophagus, intestinal canal and lymphatics of the bladder. Hence the *borborigmi*, or rumbling of the bowels, owing to their fluid contents descending as the air beneath ascends.'

The word, though, has rich application beyond the strictly medical. In Aldous Huxley's satirical novel *Point Counter Point* (1928), the ridiculous poet Willie Weaver exclaims: 'The stertorous *borborygms* of the dyspeptic Carlyle!' To which the independent-minded Lucy Tantamount responds: 'Stertorous what? Do remember that I've never been educated.' Willie does not explain, but asks instead for some brandy, almost as though he himself does not quite know what *borborygms* are.

Decacuminate

Darling, would you mind *decacuminating* that bottle? So might a thirsty logophile speak, because to *decacuminate* means, as Thomas Blount defines it, 'to take the top off any thing'. (It comes straightforwardly from the Latin, as does *decapitate*, which, strictly speaking, means taking the top off a human being.) In his later dictionary, Nathan Bailey gives the past participle *decacuminated*, 'having the Tops lopped off', but since then the word has been largely avoided. Which is a shame, because it could as well be applied to the deletion of the rude first line of an email, and many other things it is sensible to do in modern life.

It also appears in a discussion in *Plato's Introduction of Forms* (2004) by the eminent American philosopher R. M. Dancy, who was born on this day in 1938. 'Suppose you and I encountered a word quite new to both of us, say, "*decacuminate*",' he writes, 'and neither of us has the faintest notion whether this, that, or the other is *decacuminated* or not. A discussion between us of the question "What is *decacumination*?" is foredoomed to failure.' To be fair, this appearance of *decacuminate* is what linguistic philosophers would call a *mention*, but not a *use*, of the word. (Dancy holds it up for our scrutiny, but does not employ it in a sense-making way.) Still, at least we could now have that discussion.

14 December

Merrythought

George Washington died on this day in 1799, having, among other things, issued ten years earlier the first proclamation to make Thanksgiving a national holiday. A significant proportion of the people who gobble turkeys around this time of year will observe the ritual, one that goes back to classical times, of breaking the wish-bone. Technically, that is known as the *furcula*, and is where the bird's fused clavicles join, but an older and arguably finer name for it is the *merrythought*.

In the 1708 compendium of curiosities, *The British Apollo: Containing Two Thousand Answers to Curious Questions in Most Arts and Sciences*, the term is explained like this: 'For what Reason is the Bone next the Breast of a Fowl, &c. Called the *Merry-thought* ... ? The Original of that Name was doubtless from the Pleasant Fancies, that commonly arise upon the Breaking of that Bone.' How pretty. It was, then, the *merrythought* since at least the sixteenth century, while the term *wish-bone* is not recorded before 1860. Those who think that *wish-bone* is rather too grasping and covetous, then, have decent cause to revert to the traditional name.

Comperendinate

As a wise man once advised, never do today what you can put off till tomorrow. But what if tomorrow also seems frightfully soon? What you need is to *comperendinate*, which derives from the Latin for 'to put off until the third day after'. If it is Monday, and you want to delay some dull task till Thursday, it is perfect, and available.

The reader ought to be warned that, outside dictionaries, *comperendinate* mainly appears in the literary and satirical press of the nineteenth and twentieth centuries as an example of abstruse vocabulary. In 1906, a writer for *Punch* reviewed what we may assume to be an entirely imaginary work on black magic by a certain Uriburu Pangofflin, enthusing: 'M. Pangofflin, whose command of cryptic Basque places him in a position of peculiar strength as compared with other writers on the subject, appears to take the eminently common-sense view that where the *foci* in an aplanatic surface exhibit no radio-activity, it is permissible to homologate – or *comperendinate* as the Quinologists have it – a Mixo-Lydian gambit. Personally we should like to know what M. Becquerel has to say on this subject.'

Monsieur Henri Becquerel, the French physicist who shared the 1903 Nobel Prize for the discovery of radio-activity, was born on this day in 1852.

Zeugma

In his first novel, *The Posthumous Papers of the Pickwick Club* (known these days as *The Pickwick Papers*), Charles Dickens has a lot of fun with *zeugma*. 'Mr Pickwick took his hat and his leave,' we are told at one point; at another, Miss Bolo 'went straight home, in a flood of tears and a sedan-chair'. In grammar and rhetoric, *zeugma* (from the Greek for 'bond' or 'yoke') is when one verb takes two different objects (as *take* governs both *hat* and *leave*), often to comical effect. It was a favourite device in this respect of Alexander Pope: 'Here Thou, great Anna! whom three Realms obey, / Dost sometimes Counsel take – and sometimes Tea.'

Alternatively, *zeugma* can be created when two subjects incogruously share the same verb, as so magnificently illustrated in *Pride and Prejudice* by Jane Austen, who was born on this day in 1775. Elizabeth and Mr Darcy are standing on the lawn in awkward silence, and then even awkwarder small-talk, while her aunt and uncle catch up with them. Unfortunately, Austen writes, 'time and her aunt moved slowly'.

Stultiloquence

Because the Latin *stultus* means 'stupid', and *loquus* 'that which speaks', *stultiloquence* is a very satisfying word for 'stupid talk', which has not yet been eliminated from public affairs. In 1893, the poet Swinburne raged against those bad writers who were wont to 'gabble at any length like a thing most brutish in the blank and blatant jargon of epic or idyllic *stultiloquence*'. (In his 1926 book on Swinburne, Sir Harold Nicolson noted that, in this handwritten authorial addition, 'the words are written larger and larger as his excitement waxes, and the final "stultiloquence" is black and enormous, signifying a shriek of defiance'.)

Meanwhile, in a splendid essay for the *European Magazine*, dated this day of 1808, one N. Slone complains about the jargon-infested and brutish language of his day. Among many other things, Mr Slone complains about a politician having told his colleagues in the House of Commons that they were incapable of performing their duties because they had become *stultified*. The writer comments: 'This sort of epithet, so classical and appropriate when thoroughly understood through the medium of a proper vocabulary, cannot fail to add, in an eminent degree, to the *stultiloquence* of every society.' Chapeau.

Unyore

Antonio Stradivari died on this day in 1737, having not made enough instruments to satisfy the demand from violinists two centuries and more later. Many of them despise a modern instrument, even though a Stradivarius was a very modern instrument once. Such are the vagaries of time, about which it is often advisable to be vague while sounding lordly and medieval, and for such purposes the word *unyore* is a strong candidate for adoption. In that earthy, matter-of-fact, Anglo-Saxon way, it means what it looks like it should: *not yore*, i.e. 'not of ancient times', 'not long ago'. (*Yore* itself comes from Old English *geára*, the origins of which are lost in the mists of time.)

So *unyore* means 'recently' – but also, flexibly, 'soon'. Perhaps next time you are asked whether you have run a certain errand, you may reply sagely: *unyore*.

19 December

Rille

On this day in 1972, the astronauts of Apollo 17, the last Apollo mission, returned to Earth after walking among the *rilles* of the Moon. A *rille* (also spelled *rill*) is a fissure or channel on the lunar surface, often specifically a sinuous or winding channel, thought to have been created by molten lava earlier in the satellite's development. Stargazers had been observing *rilles* for more than a century before humans saw them close-up: the word's first recorded use is by a publication of the Royal Astronomical Society in 1859. Nowadays *rilles* are also seen on Mars, and many other celestial bodies too.

Borrowed from the eighteenth-century German for a furrow, *rille* is a specialized word of exogeology, also known as astrogeology or planetary geology: the study of the geology of Solar System objects besides our own planet. The Moon has also given us items of vocabulary including *graben*, for a depressed block between two faults in the crust; the rock types *norite* and *troctolite*; and the *maria*, Latin for 'seas'. The Moon doesn't have any seas, but early lunarists thought its dark basalt plains were bodies of water, and we still use the term.

Artifex

An *artifex* is the master of an art, an excellent craftsman. Initially the word served as a title for the one presumed to have crafted the whole universe. The English politician and writer Robert Mason, who died on this day in 1635, makes the first recorded use of the word in his argument for the possibility of a pious science, *Reasons Academie* (1605): 'The more nearer reason (with reverend care of its creator) searcheth into these causes, the more nearer doth it bring the soul of man to the principal *Artifex* and maker of them.'

From the Latin *ars* and *facere*, so simply 'maker of art', the word was not long limited to conceptions of the divine. Later, an *artifex* could be Nature, or a Roman emperor, or the great Louis Armstrong. When we speak of such artists, whose powers are quite out of the ordinary, let us ennoble them with the title of *artifex*.

Furibund

In Ben Jonson's satirical play *The Poetaster* – which was entered in the Stationers' Register on this day in 1601 – the bombastic *poetaster* ('bad poet') of the title, Crispinus, becomes ill and vomits up a slew of obscure long words. '*Barmy*, *froth*, *puffy*, *inflate*, *turgidous*, and *ventosity* are come up,' remarks one onlooker. 'O terrible windy words,' says a second. 'A sign of a windy brain,' adds a third sagely. And then Crispinus pukes the line: 'O – *oblatrant* – *furibund* – *fatuate* – *strenuous*.' *Oblatrant* means 'railing' or 'reviling', and was never seen again; but it is the pretty *furibund* that continued to have currency well into the late nineteenth century. From Latin *furere*, 'to rage' (and first written *furybounde* in 1490), it means 'raging' or simply 'furious'. But *furibund* (or *furibond*) sounds more severe and more splendid, especially in this quite spectacular line to be found in William Huggins and Temple Henry Croker's 1755 translation of Ariosto's *Orlando Furioso*: 'Brutal, superb, audacious, *furibond*.'

Lambent

The scientist Tiberius Cavallo, who died on this day in 1809, was the author, among other excursions in natural philosophy, of a letter read to the Royal Society in 1781 entitled 'Account of a luminous Appearance in the Heavens'. At ten o'clock one March evening, Callo had observed a dense white light in the sky forming a 'complete luminous arch from east to west'. He thought it was definitely not an appearance of the aurora borealis, since 'it eclipsed the stars over which it passed; because its light, or rather its white appearance, was stationary and not *lambent*, and because its direction was from east to west'.

Perhaps we shall never know what caused this apparition, but we do know that *lambent*, from the Latin 'to lick', originated to describe the kind of flame that dances over a surface, and then came to mean any kind of gentle light, not excluding the sort that poets see in their mistresses' eyes. A fine, soft word for a soft glow.

Rubiginous

The colour of rust being itself a beautiful one, it is a shame we have to call it either *rusty*, which makes it sound decayed, or *rust-coloured*, which is just giving up. Happily, there exists the lovely word *rubiginous*, which derives from the Latin for 'rust', *rubigo*. It is a word that has been prized by art critics and nature writers, as well as metallurgists, through the centuries. The English cleric and poet James Hurdis, who died on this day in 1801, employs it sweetly in his poem *The Favourite Village*: 'Oft as I mark upon the woody vale / The hue *rubiginous* of fast decline, / I sigh to think how soon the lovely scene / Shall pass away ...'

Abligurition

For many, this time of year is characterized mainly by a cheerful embrace of gluttony or *gulosity* (see 29 October), this first enabled by a spot of *abligurition*, which Dr Johnson defined as 'a prodigal spending on meat and drink'. The great man probably found it in the schoolmaster Nathan Bailey's *Universal Etymological English Dictionary* of 1727, where it is more colourfully given as 'a prodigal spending in Belly-Cheer'.

The word is a straight borrowing from the classical Latin *abligurire*, which means 'to squander [money] on dainties'. This goes to show that, belly-cheeringly, wantonly stuffing yourself is a great tradition throughout the history of human civilization.

Rutilant

Red candles or fairy-lights on this day will produce a soft gleaming of Christmas cheer that may be described prettily as *rutilant*. This old word comes from the Latin *rutilus*, glowing warm and red, or ruddy-golden. One medieval writer explains how to identify friendly insects thus: 'In his book sayeth of the bee Virgil, / Two kinds are, a gentil and a vile; / The gentil is small, *rutilant*, glad-cheered.' Other things described as *rutilant* down the ages are roses, repentance, the Sun, berries, a meteor's trail, and the innards of an enormous space orb.

What is *rutilant*, however, is not always comforting. In a 1917 poetical sketch of the demon Behemoth, Aldous Huxley writes: 'His eyes are little *rutilant* stones / Sunk in black basalt.' On a friendlier note, *rutilant* has also often been applied admiringly to people with red hair, who might find it altogether preferable to *ginger*.

Concupiscible

Tonight is St Stephen's Night, and this day in 1604 saw the first recorded performance of Shakespeare's *Measure for Measure*. In it, Isabella tells the Duke what Angelo had demanded of her: 'He would not but by gift of my chaste body / To his *concupiscible* intemperate lust / Release my brother.' What is *concupiscible* – from the Latin *concupiscere*, 'to aim for' or 'covet' – is characterized by intense desire, not necessarily (but often) of the sexual variety. According to the view of the human soul inherited from Plato, the rational part of our nature is joined by two irrational parts, which are the irascible (angry) and the *concupiscible*, constantly fighting against reason.

The word can also be used for the object of desire. In Laurence Sterne's *The Life and Opinions of Tristram Shandy* (1759–67), for example, the narrator explains to the 'gentle reader' why his Uncle Toby fell in love: 'For never did thy eyes behold, or thy concupiscence covet, any thing in this world more *concupiscible* than Widow Wadman.'

27 December

Fomites

Louis Pasteur, developer of germ theory, was born on this day in 1822, and it is thanks to him that we understand how infectious matter can lurk everywhere around us. The kinds of stuff it might lurk in or on are called *fomites* (pronounced FOHmiteez), which comes from the Latin for 'tinder' (so, presumably, might light a fire of illness), and it is rather disconcerting to find, in the literature, that pretty much everything can be so classed. In *Quain's Medical Dictionary* of 1882, it is stated: 'The most important *fomites* are bed-clothes, bedding, woollen garments, carpets, curtains, letters, &c.' That casual '&c', implying that the list goes on and on, is rather stylish.

Today, computer keyboards and paper money are notorious *fomites*, and we are also warned to beware of *fomites* at the dentist's or on public transport. Now wash your hands.

28 DECEMBER

Viff

The first in the series of military aircraft known as the Harrier Jump Jet, manufactured for the Royal Air Force by the British aerospace group Hawker Siddeley, made its maiden flight on this day in 1967. Because its engines could swivel from a vertical to a horizontal orientation, it was able to take off vertically (hence 'jump') and then fly forwards: it was a VTOL (Vertical Take-Off and Landing) aircraft. This capability also gave rise to the verb *viff* – and if that sounds speedy and flexible, it's quite appropriate. It first appears in a 1972 article about the Harrier in *Flight International* magazine, which notes that the plane's swivelling engines enable it to 'vector its thrust', i.e. point it in different directions, so for example stopping in mid-air to veer abruptly sideways. This, the writer noted, demonstrated the 'possibilities of VIFF (vectoring in forward flight)'.

Soon the word lost its capitals and *viffing* was just what Harriers and related aircraft did. Beyond the world of military-pilot slang, we could profitably adopt *viff* – 'to change direction abruptly' (*OED*) – to the sudden about-turns of sly politicians.

Onomatomania

You know the feeling of not being able to remember the word for something? If, in particular, you can't remember the word for not being able to remember the word for something, then you are suffering *onomatomania* with respect to *onomatomania*, for that is what it means. Or one of its meanings, anyway: the word – from the Greek for 'name madness' – was first defined in *The New Sydenham Society's Lexicon of Medicine and the Allied Sciences* (1892) as both 'intense mental anguish at the inability to recall some word or name a thing' and also 'morbid dread of some word'.

Later, it was also used to mean an irrational obsession with words themselves. William Osler, a Canadian physician who was one of the founding professors of Johns Hopkins Hospital, and who died on this day in 1919, spoke that year to an audience of classicists, aiming to show how their discipline was much loved and used even in science, for had not everything in botany and medicine been given a classical name? 'Within the narrow compass of the primitive cell from which all living beings originate,' he said, for example, '*onomatomania* runs riot,' and then reeled off a passage of Greek-derived technical terminology. If the present book, too, is an example of *onomatomania* in this sense, so be it.

Grimalkin

In Shakespeare's *Macbeth*, one of the witches cries: 'I come, Gray-Malkin!', this being the name of her familiar, a cat inhabited by a malicious spirit. But *Gray-Malkin* was a common affectionate name for cats, even though a *malkin* was a crude mop made from rags, and the name was often used by admirers of the animal, so that *grimalkin* came to be a fond synonym for 'cat'. Here is the poet John Philips, born on this day in 1676, in his burlesque poem *Splendid Shilling*: '*Grimalkin*, to domestic vermine sworn / An everlasting foe, with watchful eye / Lies nightly brooding o'er a chinky gap, / Protending her fell claws, to thoughtless mice / Sure ruin.'

31 DECEMBER

Callithumpian

What's that racket? If it's positively *callithumpian*, it comes from a group of people playing instruments or banging on cans to make a cacophonous noise. In nineteenth-century America, a *callithumpian* band was the cause of uproarious street revelry, and a '*callithumpian* serenade' made 'night hideous'; thenceforth, any kind of ugly noise could be termed *callithumpian*. (The word is thought to come from late eighteenth-century southern England, where a society of social reformers known as the *Gallithumpians*, who dressed in ragged coats, were wont to cause a rumpus on election days.)

In 1859, the American linguist John Russell Bartlett explained: 'It was a common practice in New York, as well as other parts of the country, on New Year's Eve, for persons to assemble with tin horns, bells, rattles, and similar euphonious instruments, and parade the streets, making all the noise and discord possible. This party was called the *Callithumpians*, or the *Callithumpian* band. Fortunately the custom has now fallen almost, if not entirely, into disuse.' If only he knew. Happy New Year to one and all.

Sources

Examples of word usage in plays, novels, magazines, and so forth are generally sourced in the text: in old quotations I have lightly modernized the spelling for ease of reading. The major dictionaries consulted are as follows:

1538: Thomas Elyot, *The Dictionary of Syr Thomas Eliot Knyght*

1565: Thomas Cooper, *Thesaurus Linguae Romanae et Britannicae*

1604: Robert Cawdrey, *A Table Alphabeticall*

1623: Henry Cockeram, *The English Dictionary; or, An Interpreter of Hard English Words*

1656: Thomas Blount, *Glossographia*

1658: Edward Phillips, *The New World of English Words*

1670: Thomas Blount, *Nomo-Lexicon*

1674: John Ray, *A Collection of English Words Not Generally Used*

1702: John Kersey, *A New English Dictionary*

1706: John Kersey and Edward Phillips: *The New World of Words: Or, Universal English Dictionary*

1721: Nathan Bailey, *Universal Etymological English Dictionary*

1728: Ephraim Chambers, *Cyclopaedia, or an Universal Dictionary of Arts and Sciences*

1730: Nathan Bailey, *Dictionarium Britannicum*

1755: Samuel Johnson, *Dictionary of the English Language*

1775: John Ash, *A New and Complete Dictionary of the English Language*

1794: Hester Lynch Piozzi, *British Synonymy*

1796: Francis Grose, *Classical Dictionary of the Vulgar Tongue*

1820: Richard Paul Jodrell, *Philology of the English Language*

1825: John Jamieson, *Etymological Dictionary of the Scottish Language*

1828: Noah Webster, *American Dictionary of the English Language.*

1859: John Camden Hotten, *Dictionary of Modern Slang, Cant and Vulgar Words*

1884 to the present: James Murray et. al., *Oxford English Dictionary*

Acknowledgements

The author wishes to thank the eximious Jane Sturrock, Charlotte Fry, Ella Patel, Nick de Somogyi, and John Elek. Very special thanks, meanwhile, to Vicky and Fox. Go team!

Acknowledgments

Steven Poole is the author of *Rethink*, *Unspeak*, and other books. He writes the 'Word of the Week' column in the *Guardian*, and essays and reviews for many publications.